THE MODERN NATIONS IN
HISTORICAL PERSPECTIVE

ROBIN W. WINKS, *General Editor*

The volumes in this series deal with individual
nations or groups of closely related nations
throughout the world, summarizing the chief historical trends and influences that have contributed
to each nation's present-day character, problems,
and behavior. Recent data are incorporated with
established historical background to achieve a
fresh synthesis and original interpretation.

RONALD H. CHILCOTE, the author of this volume,
is a graduate of Dartmouth College and obtained
his Ph.D. at Stanford University. A Fellow of the
African Studies Association, he is presently As-
sistant Professor of Political Science at the University of California, Riverside. His publications
include the forthcoming *Emerging Portuguese
African Nationalism* and various articles in scholarly journals.

ALSO IN THE AFRICAN SUBSERIES

Central Africa *by Prosser Gifford*
The Congo *by Harry R. Rudin*
Egypt & the Sudan *by Robert O. Collins & Robert L. Tignor*
Ethiopia, Eritrea & the Somalilands *by William H. Lewis*
Morocco, Algeria, Tunisia *by Richard M. Brace*
Nigeria & Ghana *by John E. Flint*
Sierra Leone & Liberia *by Christopher Fyfe*
West Africa: The Former French States *by John D. Hargreaves*

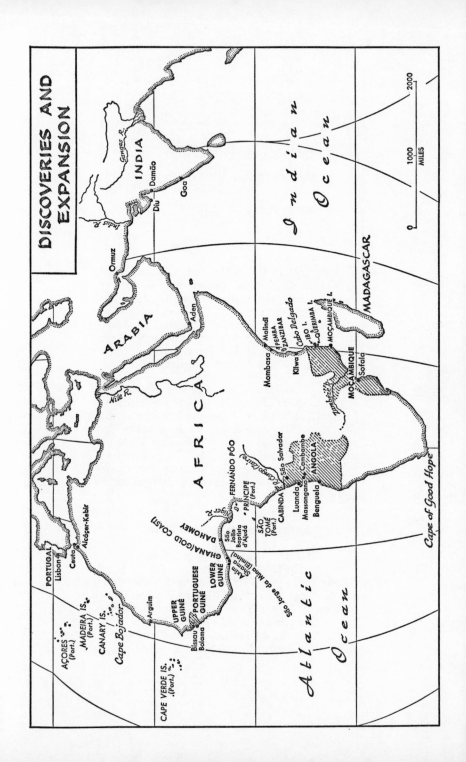

DISCOVERIES AND EXPANSION

PORTUGAL
Lisbon
Ceuta
Alcázar-Kebir

AÇORES
(Port.)
MADEIRA IS.
(Port.)
CANARY IS.
Cape Bojador

CAPE VERDE IS.
(Port.)

Arguim

UPPER GUINÉ

PORTUGUESE
GUINÉ
Bissau
Bolama
LOWER
GUINÉ
Niger R.
São João
Baptista
d'Ajudá
Axim
Shama
GHANA(GOLD COAST)
DAHOMEY
São Jorge da Mina (Elmina)

FERNANDO PÓO
PRÍNCIPE (Port.)
SÃO TOMÉ (Port.)

AFRICA

Nile R.

ARABIA

Aden

Ormuz

INDIA

Indus R.

Ganges R.

Diu
Damão
Goa

Indian Ocean

Atlantic Ocean

CABINDA
Congo (Zaire)
São Salvador
Luanda
Massangano
Cambambe
ANGOLA
Benguela

Mombasa
Malindi
PEMBA
ZANZIBAR
Kilwa
Cabo Delgado
IBO I.
QUERIMBA I.
MOÇAMBIQUE I.
MOÇAMBIQUE
Zambézi
Sofala

MADAGASCAR

Cape of Good Hope

0   1000   2000
MILES

PORTUGUESE AFRICA

Ronald H. Chilcote

A SPECTRUM BOOK

Prentice-Hall, Inc.

Englewood Cliffs, New Jersey

For Frances, Stephen, and Edward

The present volume represents a synthesis of developments in the Portuguese possessions of Africa. An introductory chapter focuses on the tradition of empire that to a large extent has shaped the pattern of Portuguese activity in Africa during the past five hundred years. Portuguese colonial policy is examined through historical periods of success and failure, namely discoveries, conquest, pacification, and colonization. A second chapter delineates the basic problems that beset both Portugal and Portuguese Africa today. Institutional forces are examined in depth to evaluate the strengths and weaknesses that allow for continued Portuguese domination and influence in Africa or for the independence of the African possessions. The third chapter differentiates between prevailing Portuguese and African conceptions of nationalism and development and serves as a framework for succeeding chapters which concentrate on political, economic, social, and cultural trends in each territory. Since most of the available literature reflects an exaggerated view of Portugal's role in Africa, an attempt has been made to present a balanced account of the basic forces that shape life in each territory. A concluding chapter summarizes the contemporary situation and offers perspectives on the area as a whole.

Research was undertaken in Portugal during 1960 and 1961 as well as during a field trip to Africa in 1965. The Portuguese do not welcome research and scholarship by those who are unwilling to support the official position and policy in Africa. Travel to the overseas possessions is severely restricted. Desiring interviews and information from Portuguese officials, I was granted visas to visit Angola and Moçambique during July 1965. The Portuguese secret police, however, seized me as I deplaned in Luanda. I was interrogated, mainly on the subject matter of the present book, held incommunicado in prison for six days, and finally released after field notes and part of the book manuscript had been confiscated.

In spite of my recent experience, my investigation has been assisted by Portuguese and Africans alike. I am particularly grateful for permission to research materials in many of Lisbon's archives and libraries, especially in the Biblioteca Nacional, the Instituto Superior de Estudos Ultramarinos, the Arquivo Nacional da Torre do Tombo, the Arquivo Histórico Ultramarino, and the Sociedade de Geografia de Lisboa. I have extensively consulted the Portuguese collection of the Harvard University Library as well as the collection on nineteenth and twentieth century economic and political history of Portuguese Africa in the libraries of Stanford University and the Hoover Institution on War, Revolution, and Peace.

Portuguese orthography is confused by many revisions since the fifteenth century discoveries in Africa, and I have attempted to retain the usage of a particular period. Also I have used the Portuguese form of most African proper names and generally have included the African spelling in parentheses.

I wish to acknowledge financial support for this and related study of Portuguese Africa. I am particularly grateful to the Hoover Institution, which has made available funds to collect documents issued by Portuguese African nationalist groups, and to Dr. Peter Duignan of the Institute for his generous assistance, advice, and support of my investigations. A University of California Faculty Fellowship provided me with time for field research and writing, and a University intramural research grant supported research assistance and manuscript typing.

I wish to thank Miss Hildeliza Arias for her excellent typing of the various manuscript drafts. Finally, I am deeply indebted to Professors James Duffy of Brandeis University, Immanuel Wallerstein of Columbia University, Douglas Wheeler of the University of New Hampshire, Robin Winks, and my wife, Frances Bunker Chilcote, for their incisive and thoughtful comments, criticisms, and editing.

R. H. C.

Contents

ONE   Imperial Success and Failure   1

Discoveries and Expansion, 3; Attempts at Consolidation, 6; The Decline of Influence, 9; Colonial Policy, 14

TWO   Institutional Forces and Change   21

Structural Problems, 21; Supports and Countersupports, 30; A Framework for Change, 40

THREE   Nationalism and Development   43

Portuguese Nationalism, 45; Lusotropicology: A Defense of the Portuguese Position, 47; African Nationalism, 49

FOUR   Angola   53

Fragmentation and Disruption, 55; The Rise and Fall of the Congo Monarchy, 61; The Conquest of the Angolan Kingdoms, 65; The Benguela Highlands and the Native Resistance to the South, 71; Nationalist Rebellion in the 1960's, 74

FIVE   Portuguese Guiné, the Cape Verde Archipelago, and São Tomé and Príncipe   83

The Historical Perspective, 86; Ethnographic Conflict, 89; Economic Stagnation, 91; African Resistance and Nationalist Ideals, 93

SIX   Moçambique   105

Economic Weaknesses, 107; Social and Cultural Differentiation, 108; Early Historical Patterns, 111; Pacification and Discontent, 115;
Nationalism and the Independence Struggle,
118

SEVEN   Prospect and Retrospect   123

A Set of Propositions, 123; Perspectives, 126

Suggested Readings   129

Index   143

Maps

Discoveries and Expansion, Frontispiece; An-
gola, 54; Portuguese Guiné, the Cape Verde
Islands, and São Tomé and Príncipe, 84;
Moçambique, 106

ONE

IMPERIAL SUCCESS AND FAILURE

The Portuguese territories of Angola, Guiné and the Cape Verde islands, Moçambique, and São Tomé and Príncipe are not independent nations seeking their own course in the contemporary world. Officially these African territories are Portugal's "overseas provinces" which are integrated politically, socially, and economically with the motherland. In practice, the Portuguese African possessions are colonies dominated by a forty-year-old dictatorial order. In fact, the African colonies cannot be viewed as "modern" in outlook and development, for rapid and substantial progress, reform, social change, and development have not been the manifestations of that order.

Backwardness and authoritarianism are traditional manifestations of the Portuguese political order. In October 1910 a republic was proclaimed as an alternative to authoritarian rule under a monarchy that had dominated nearly eight centuries. But reforms came slowly, and the aspirations of the expectant masses diminished as republican Portugal failed to correct economic weaknesses, social ills, and widespread illiteracy, and to constitute a viable polity. Caught between a self-interested oligarchy of landowners, military officers, clergy, and others on the one hand, and the alienated poverty-stricken masses of peasants and workers on the other, the Republic faltered as strikers and a deteriorating financial situation prompted the new order to succumb to tradition. Dictatorial order was established briefly by a military figure, Sidónio Pais, in December 1917. Soon after, Pais was assassinated, and republican power shifted from faction to faction as cabinets incessantly fell before a welter of strikes, riots, and mutinies in the army and navy. By 1925 a Portuguese bank scandal had lowered the Republic's prestige still further.

On May 28, 1926, the army, always eager to intervene in politics, abruptly ended the republican experiment and brought Portugal full circle to an era of authoritarianism. Probably influenced by the success of Benito Mussolini, who overthrew the Italian government in 1922, and Miguel

Primo de Rivera, who seized power in Spain a year later, General Manuel Gomes da Costa, commanding the garrison at Braga, proclaimed a revolt, marched on Lisbon, and established a military triumvirate. Six weeks later General António Oscar de Fragoso Carmona seized undisputed control of the government and proclaimed a military dictatorship. In May 1928 António de Oliveira Salazar, an economics professor at the University of Coimbra, accepted the post of finance minister and soon after succeeded in balancing the national budget, winning concessions, and gradually consolidating power until by 1933 he had drawn up a colonial act and a new constitution under which Portugal was proclaimed the "New State."

Under Salazar major attention focused on the African colonies through the exaggerated propagation of Portugal's imperial mystique premised upon the great exploits of Portuguese discovery and expansion during the fifteenth and sixteenth centuries. Several developments foreshadowed an end to that imperial mystique, however. At home the regime found itself challenged in 1958 by presidential candidate and former Salazar supporter Humberto Delgado, who vigorously denounced the long-lived dictatorial order and awakened many Portuguese to the possibility of new political alternatives.

In Africa, emergent nationalism represented the greatest challenge, being manifested after the early 1961 seizure of the luxury liner "Santa Maria" by a former colonial officer, Henrique Galvão. This event precipitated an African outbreak in Luanda in February and a widespread uprising throughout large areas of northern Angola a month later. Prompted perhaps by the early success of the guerrilla war in Angola, nationalists in Portuguese Guiné launched their struggle for independence in 1962. Two years later Moçambique nationalists opened up their military offensive.

In such circumstances, Portugal's economy labored under the burden of maintaining thousands of troops on African soil. With some forty per cent of the annual budget allocated to the military and the colonial wars in Africa, an urgent question became how long the mother country would be willing and able to afford this burden. Uncertain about the attitude of the metropole toward the African possessions, Portuguese colonial residents sought closer political and economic ties with South Africa and Southern Rhodesia.

Additionally, Portuguese prestige suffered from attacks by the United Nations and other international organizations. In November 1960 the U.N. Trusteeship Committee censured Portugal as "a menace to peace" for refusing to submit annual reports on its "dependent" areas. A few months later, on March 15, 1961, the day on which rebellion exploded in northern

Angola, the Security Council debated a resolution demanding an inquiry into disorders that had taken place in Angola. A week later the General Assembly voted in favor of debating the Angola question, and in April it resolved that Portugal undertake reforms in the territory. In November the Trusteeship Committee censured Portugal for refusing to report on its overseas possessions, and a month later a similar resolution was approved in the General Assembly. In January 1962 the General Assembly affirmed the "right of the Angolan people to self-determination and independence."

Portugal moved to allay international protest over colonial administration and policy by announcing a series of reform measures and appealing for the support of its fellow members of the North Atlantic Treaty Organization (NATO), especially the United States, which maintained strategic military bases on the Açores. Nevertheless, debate on Portuguese Africa continued throughout 1963 and 1964. In November 1965 the Security Council approved a compromise resolution that Portugal grant self-determination to its African territories and that all member nations withhold from Portugal any assistance which would allow continued repression in the territories. A stronger resolution urging members to break diplomatic and commercial relations with Portugal was passed a month later by the General Assembly.

Discoveries and Expansion

Portugal's contemporary problems in Africa stem from the past, beginning with the great exploits of the fifteenth and sixteenth centuries. Having successfully expelled the Moors from national territory in the thirteenth century, a unified Portugal turned its attention to dreams of expansion and conquest. The inertia of Portugal's crusading ardor against the Moors prompted a desire to fulfill its imperial destiny. The capture of Ceuta in 1415 provided the bridgehead and access to northern Africa and the hinterland beyond as well as control of the terminal point for the trans-Sahara gold trade.

The Portuguese imperial design owes its conception to the ambitions and early achievements of Prince Henry "the Navigator," the third son of King João I. According to the chronicler, Azurara, Henry's motives were fivefold: First, to expore the unknown country beyond Cape Bojador; second, to establish commercial ties with any Christian nations discovered; third, to determine the extent of Mohammedan influence in the unknown African lands; fourth, to seek Christian allies to help against the enemy; and fifth, to win new Christian converts. With the passage of time and preliminary explorations, Portuguese objectives focused on control of the

Guiné gold trade, Negro slaves, the spices of the Far East, and the quest for the Christian kingdom of Prester John.

Prince Henry devoted his energies to organizing the systematic exploration of the west coast of Africa from 1415 until his death in 1460. Although the islands of Madeira and perhaps the Açores probably had been sighted by forgotten Catalan or Italian wanderers of the thirteenth or fourteenth centuries, they were uninhabited until the Portuguese discovery and colonization of Madeira in 1418-1420 and that of the Açores a decade later. By 1434 Portuguese ships had rounded Cape Bojador, and in 1441 the island of Arguim just south of Cape Blanco was discovered. Arguim became a base for the inland trade and for the fishing fleets that began to exploit the rich fishing grounds off the coast. About 1445 the area known today as Portuguese Guiné was reached, and the Cape Verdes were discovered before 1460. Thereafter, the Portuguese concentrated on exploiting the few commodities desired by Europe, namely slaves, pepper, ivory, and gold. In particular, the West African gold interested Western Europe, whose wares were becoming increasingly costly and precious metals scarce. To consolidate their hold on the African coastal trade, the Portuguese built the castle of São Jorge da Mina on the island of Elmina.

While attention focused on trade, only small areas of West Africa were actually settled by the Portuguese between the fifteenth and twentieth centuries. Influence in Upper Guiné (roughly the coastal area from Cape Blanco to Sierra Leone) was slight. North of the Senegal river Moslem merchants dominated most of the trade, and the Portuguese permanent settlement at Arguim was allowed to fall into decline. South of the Senegal, Portuguese influence was greater and extended inland via the good river routes of the Senegal and the Gambia. Off the coast the Cape Verde islands served as a Portuguese colonial base offering ready access for the penetration of the mainland. In Lower Guiné (from Sierra Leone to the Cameroons) the Portuguese had little contact with the Grain Coast (corresponding to Liberia today and so named because of its principal export, pepper) and the Ivory Coast, mainly because they lacked natural harbors and frequent storms made it unsafe for sailing ships to station close to them for lengthy periods of time. In contrast, the Gold Coast (present-day Ghana) was the center of Portuguese commercial activity. Besides its castle at Elmina, Portugal built forts at Axim and Shama. Activity there, however, was limited to the extensive gold trade with the coastal peoples who actively opposed and prevented Portuguese attempts to establish direct trade links with the interior. Along the Slave Coast (between the Volta river and the Niger delta) there was little gold and consequently little Portuguese effort to establish permanent influence with the coastal natives. At Benin, however, a trading post was erected to take advantage of the slave and pepper trade. Later Benin was abandoned in favor of the islands of São Tomé, Fernando Póo and Príncipe, which the Portuguese began to settle at the end of the fifteenth century and where sugar planters enjoyed great prosperity until about 1570, when a part of the slave population became uncontrollable. At the same time, Northeast Brazil appeared economically more attractive.

With the discovery of these islands in the Gulf of Guiné, Portuguese explorers moved southward. Diogo Cão arrived at the mouth of the Zaire or Congo river in 1482 or 1483 and discovered the kingdom of the Mani-congo. A second voyage took him along the coast of present-day Angola. Finally, during a voyage of 1487-1488, Bartolomeu Dias rounded the Cape of Good Hope, thereby opening up the trade route to the riches of the East.

At about the same time, Pero de Covilhã set out on an exploratory mis-sion, crossed the Mediterranean, advanced down the Red Sea, and even-tually reached the Persian gulf and the Malabar coast of India. Later his journey also took him down the eastern coast of Africa, perhaps as far south as Sofala and certainly to the highlands of Ethiopia in search of Prester John, the mysterious prince of Christian faith.

Immediately more attention was paid to East than to West Africa, principally because it was necessary to hold several strong points along the coast to secure the route to India and secondarily because commercial ties with the interior had already been established by Arab traders who occupied important coastal centers. King Manuel's plan was to send Vasco da Gama to India. Setting out in 1497, Gama rounded the Cape and landed at the mouth of the Quelimane river, where he came in contact with hostile Arab trading vessels. Moving up the coast, the expedition was nearly destroyed at Mombasa but escaped to Malindi, a point further north along the Kenyan coast where the Portuguese were treated well. From there he reached Calicut on the Malabar coast.

The Portuguese next turned to the task of empire-building. By 1505 they had gained supremacy over the trade of the Indian Ocean and had made satellites of minor Indian states. In that year Francisco de Almeida was named viceroy and ordered to pursue a comprehensive plan for ensur-ing Portuguese supremacy in the Indian Ocean. His objective was the establishment of military settlements at strategic points from southeast Africa to southwest India. In Africa, Sofala was occupied, and the con-struction of a Portuguese fort assured control of the gold trade. The island of Moçambique was captured and fortified. Other strategic points occupied by the Portuguese were Kilwa and Mombasa. By 1509 Almeida had defeated the allied naval force of Egypt and the Sultanate of Gujarat at Diu in India. His victory assured Portuguese naval supremacy over the Indian Ocean for nearly a century.

Almeida was replaced by Affonso de Albuquerque whose principal objective was to take possession of several strong central positions (a policy opposed by Almeida) and to secure the foundations of the Portuguese empire. Goa was captured in 1510 and quickly became the capital of the eastern conquests. A year later Malacca was taken and the spice trade secured. Albuquerque next determined to gain control of the Red Sea trade. In 1513 his fleet was beaten off at Aden, but two years later, just before his death, Albuquerque seized Ormuz where he erected a fort.

The exploits of Almeida and Albuquerque fulfilled the Portuguese dream of conquest and imperial expansion. In little more than a century Portugal had become a world power whose supremacy extended westward to Brazil and along the coast of Africa from Ceuta to the Red Sea while the Asian dominions spread from Ormuz in the Persian Gulf to India, Ceylon, and Malacca. Only Aden remained unconquered. Albuquerque's successor failed in a second attempt to overcome that strategic point. Thus the Red Sea trade route remained open and, according to the historian, Charles Nowell, the Portuguese thereafter never gained full mastery of the situation.

Attempts at Consolidation

The tightening of its hold over the African possessions was a multifold task for the Portuguese whose mission involved instilling Christian ideals in the "uncivilized" masses, expanding influence into the unknown interior, conquering the native populations with wars of "pacification," and encouraging white Portuguese to settle in the colonial areas.

In the Cape Verdes, uninhabited until the Portuguese arrival, feudal practices were applied by the crown, which granted whole islands or parts of islands to proprietors who managed the settlers brought from Portugal and slaves from West Africa. The islands became not only a center of colonial activity but the link between the European homeland and other colonial possessions to the south and east.

What little attention was directed to Guiné tended to focus on economic matters, since the Portuguese objective was to obtain a firm hold on the coastal trade and to dominate a considerable portion of the gold supply. Inland Portuguese influence was limited by the difficulties of penetrating the barriers of the coastal forest, surviving the rugged tropics, and overcoming the hostility of the Moslem traders who dominated commercial activity. Thus the Portuguese were more interested in trade than in encouraging settlement of large expanses of West Africa. The areas they ruled and settled were small and were typically concentrated at coastal points or on offshore islands.

An experiment was attempted south of the Congo river where the Portuguese discovered the Kingdom of the Congo. There they convinced the rulers of the African regime to adopt Christianity. The African king took the name of Affonso I and became Christian and an advocate of European civilization. During his reign, Affonso carried on with the task of creating a Christian state with a political and social system molded to the European model of the time. The Portuguese strategy was not to secure control of the kingdom but to treat Affonso and his native subjects as allies. Although the Portuguese left a cultural imprint that was to endure for some time, their experiment collapsed as the attention of the Portuguese kings was diverted more and more from Africa. Nevertheless, in spite of the opposition of Africans and the rude behavior of the Portuguese colonialists, Portugal continued to lend political support to Affonso's successors. Located at São Salvador, these rulers generally endorsed the Portuguese cause. During the last years of the royal dynasty, Portugal selected António III, a Catholic, thus alienating Protestant Africans living in the former Belgian Congo. These Africans established a nationalist movement and launched open rebellion in northern Angola in March 1961, thereby shattering the Portuguese dream of implanting Lusitanian civilization upon that portion of Africa.

Further south, there were persistent efforts to convert and "civilize" the natives of Angola and Benguela, but the African natives were considered to be "barbarous" savages whose conversion was dependent on methods of force rather than persuasion. It was not unusual, therefore, for the early colonial officials to press for full-scale colonization of at least part of Angola by peasant families from Portugal. This idea was abandoned as attention concentrated on the lucrative slave trade. Instead of colonization, a system of *donatárias* (territorial proprietorship) was established as a sixteenth-century practice. Originating in Portuguese medieval feudal organization, the system gave to proprietors favored by the crown the right to administrative jurisdiction over large expanses of land in exchange for the responsibility to defend and settle that land. Centuries later the Salazar regime seriously revived the idea of encouraging Portuguese peasant families to migrate to Angola. The purpose was threefold: to achieve cultural integration, to relieve internal Portuguese problems of overpopulation and economic poverty, and to ensure political hegemony.

The two principal colonization schemes in Angola were for white settlers. The first was at Cela, located between Luanda and Nova Lisboa. There the settler could not use native African labor; each was given 150 acres of land and, lent over a twenty-five year period, a house, some farm equipment, seeds, and two oxen. A second project was located near Matala in southern Angola. Unlike Cela, which is far from any form of transportation, Matala has ready access to markets and draws upon a nearby hydroelectric dam which provides electricity and irrigation. Both projects proved costly to the government and demonstrated limited success, owing to the lack of initiative and the inexperience of the poor and badly educated Portuguese settlers.

Moçambique's first settlement was established at Sofala. From there a chain of forts was extended northward along the Moçambique, Tanganyika, and Kenya coasts. The object of this activity was to obtain control of the eastern trade passing through the Red Sea and to divert it to a Portuguese route around southern Africa, thereby escaping the heavy Middle East tolls levied on trade destined for Europe. Occupation of East Africa thus was limited to strategically scattered points along the coast.

During the seventeenth century a few expeditions moved inland in search of the gold mines of the African "empire" of Monomotapa. A settlement scheme, proposed in 1635, aimed at opening up the river commerce and exploiting the gold trade but was bypassed in favor of sending an expedition of settlers to India. In 1677 another settlement scheme failed to materialize. Throughout the century Portugal continued to neglect the East African possessions for the riches of India and the Far East. Earlier, the acquisition of Portugal by Spain (during 1580-1640) had led to a decline in Portuguese sea power, however, and colonies were increasingly exposed to the attacks of the Dutch and English. East Africa no longer remained subject to Portuguese rule alone.

Portuguese attempts to consolidate a hold on Moçambique were hindered by an unwillingness to develop the territory. Merchants traded in slaves with Brazil, the enterprise becoming important in the nineteenth century. Efforts to settle the territory focused on the system of *prazos* (a modification of the *donatária* system) or land concessions whereby large estates were settled by owners authorized by the crown of Portugal. In theory, the *prazos* were to be given to the wife of a white couple and held in the female line for three generations after which the *prazos* would revert to the crown. Actually, half-caste women and men came to own most of the *prazos* of the Zambeze river valley and elsewhere. Throughout the seventeenth to nineteenth centuries this system was greatly abused. The owners of the concessions illegally extended their territory beyond the assigned limits, failed to encourage colonization or cultivation of the land, and refused to pay tribute to the crown while at the same time extracting payment from or forcing into slavery the native subjects. Additionally, the *prazo* system was weakened by absentee holders who tended to reside in Brazil or Goa.

Economic development continued to lag by the end of the nineteenth century. Lacking the financial resources for such development, Portugal adopted an English and Dutch experiment and introduced the system of chartered companies. In 1891 the northern district of Cabo Delgado was granted to the Niassa Company, and an area between the Save and Zambeze rivers was handed over to the Moçambique Company. A year later another region was conceded to the Zambézia Company.

Substantial development failed to materialize, however. In the 1950's the Salazar government initiated a colonization program in the Limpopo valley. Some six thousand people, including Africans and Europeans, were settled. The settlers were to work their own land, and hired labor was forbidden. Unlike the European, the African was not housed and received a land concession about half the size of the European farmer. The project proved costly and was limited by the large numbers of illiterate and unskilled Portuguese peasants brought by the government. The government, however, persisted in encouraging an increase of settlement "for the national defense" of Moçambique. While acknowledging that the settlement boards established in 1961 had failed to modify substantially the unbalanced ratio of whites to blacks, the government attempted to stem the tide of legal and illegal emigration of tens of thousands of Portuguese to other European countries. The excessive cost of more than $10,000 to settle a single family in Africa was proving prohibitive to a government which also faced heavy expenditure in the military struggle against Moçambique nationalists.

The Decline of Influence

Charles Nowell notes in *A History of Portugal* that a "combination of luck, geographic position, maritime skill, and native daring had given the Portuguese a lead they could not hold long." August 1578, when King Sebastião led his army to disastrous defeat at Alcácer-Kebir, marked the turning point in Portuguese imperial destiny. Sebastião moved inland from Arzilla, only to be overcome by the Moslems who resisted his advance.

The king's death led to the seizure in 1580 of the Portuguese crown by King Felipe II of Spain and to sixty years under Spanish rule which witnessed a lessening of Portuguese overseas activity and the exhaustion of naval resources.

Having achieved separation from Spain in 1640, Portugal attempted the work of reconstruction. The main problem was an impassioned evocation of the glorious past and insistence on maintaining colonial commitments to three continents. The Portuguese fleet had suffered severely from participation in Felipe's Armada in 1588. At the same time they were challenged by the sea power of the Dutch, English, and French. The success of Dutch expansion during the first half of the seventeenth century was based on superior manpower and economic resources. The Dutch concentrated on the Portuguese possessions everywhere—in Asia, Africa, and South America. The struggle for the spice trade of Asia resulted in victory for the Dutch, who established control in Java, seized Malacca, and took Portuguese settlements in Ceylon. In Brazil, part of the Northeast remained in Dutch control until their expulsion in 1654. The struggle in Africa resulted in a draw. In West Africa the Dutch established themselves on the Guiné coast, and in 1638 they succeeded in capturing the fortress of São Jorge da Mina. Three years later they temporarily occupied the coast of Angola. In East Africa, by contrast, the Dutch failed to seize the island of Moçambique.

Among other important causes of the decline was the absence of a comprehensive scheme of colonial administration and settlement. Relations with the African natives and Arab traders deteriorated as monopolization of commerce was maintained. Without financial resources, economic development was impossible, especially since little intensive effort was directed at exploiting mineral resources and agricultural commodities or at establishing industry in the colonies. The empire itself was to prove a substantial liability and a drain on Portugal's resources.

Unable to mobilize economic resources, the Portuguese also suffered from a backward system of centralized colonial decision-making and policy formation. Royal decision and policies emanated from Lisbon while the colonial bureaucracy at home and in the colonies experienced difficulty in implementation not only because of frequent political instability but also because of a lack of financial resources and competent personnel. Appointment to colonial service was based on a system of patronage and graft, and colonial administrators were intolerably incompetent. Furthermore, the lack of a large and solid middle class contributed to Portugal's inability to bear the burden of managing the empire.

Perhaps the greatest cause of the decay of the Portuguese colonies centered on the question of slavery, for the demoralizing impact of slavery upon both trader and slave was a retarding factor which resulted in the neglect of economic development and effective colonization of the African territories. In East Africa during the fifteenth and sixteenth centuries, the Portuguese were principally interested in exploiting the gold and ivory trade while using slaves as domestic servants. In Guiné and Angola, however, slave trading was prevalent.

The tradition of relegating the black African to inferior status prevails today. The slave's existence was miserable; the point need not be stressed. The average life of a slave on a plantation or in a mine generally is estimated at from seven to ten years. The Portuguese tolerance of slavery belies the claim that they had no color bar, a claim which Charles Boxer affirms "cannot be substantiated," nor can the view be supported that the Portuguese have promoted racial harmony, for the demand for slaves simultaneously intensified intertribal wars and hatred for the white rulers.

Miscegenation between white and black resulted in the creation of a thoroughly Portuguese mulatto population on the Cape Verdes and on São Tomé and Príncipe. The island of Santiago in the Cape Verdes and São Tomé became centers where slaves from Guiné were collected and held until sent to the plantations and mines of South America. Along the coast, Arguim became a major slave center. During the seventeenth century the slave trade shifted from the Cape Verdes to other centers, in Angola and Benguela in particular, although the discovery of gold in Brazil made it necessary for the Portuguese to seek Negro slaves along the Guiné coast who were considered to be stronger and better fitted for mining work than the natives from Angola. The Guiné coast therefore prospered from the slave trade from roughly 1650 to 1800.

In contrast to the west coast of Africa, Portuguese commerce on the east coast initially concentrated on gold and ivory. Until the eighteenth century slaves were used only as domestic servants. Thereafter, they were exported in larger numbers to America, although the total involved never reached the level exported from Guiné and Angola.

The myth of racial harmony in the African territories has its basis in the fact that the Portuguese male freely mated with colored women, yet Portugal's concentration on the slave trade was rooted in the belief that the African Negro could be legitimately enslaved. Even today, affirms James Duffy, the African's relationship with the Portuguese remains the same—that of a servant. Furthermore, the Portuguese considered the African inferior to white men. This is made indisputably clear in the literature of the Portuguese writers whose deeply rooted conviction of white superiority has lasted for centuries and is shared by other Latin writers as well as Anglo-Saxons, despite sporadic efforts by humanitarians and liberals to combat it.

The persistence of such racial prejudice and the treatment of the African Negro led several writers to condemn the Portuguese role in Africa. Criticism of slavery was frequent within Portugal itself, prompting the Marquês de Sá da Bandeira to initiate elaborate antislavery legislation in 1836. In practice, however, slavery remained in effect long thereafter. In 1858 a decree provided for the gradual abolition of slavery within twenty years throughout the empire. Slaves became *libertos* (free but obliged to work for their former masters) until the first Portuguese native labor code was implemented in 1875. Under this colonial legislation, nonproductive Africans frequently were judged vagrants and forced to contract for their services. Malpractices and exploitation continued, preventing a free labor market.

The strongest protest of improper labor conditions in Portuguese Africa emanated from important Englishmen. In 1906 a well-known and popular journalist, Henry W. Nevinson, published A *Modern Slavery* which passionately documented—in the tradition of nineteenth century antislavery literature—the slave-labor practices denied by many Portuguese apologists. Basing his report on interviews during a 1904-1905 visit to Portuguese Africa, Nevinson succeeded in arousing public sentiment against the "legalized slavery" in São Tomé and Angola. He estimated "at least half the population as living under some form of slavery—either in family slavery to natives, or general slavery to white men, or in plantation slavery." He urged that English chocolate manufacturers boycott the cocoa of São Tomé. William Cadbury, of the Cadbury Brothers chocolate firm, later visited the Portuguese possessions and in his *Labour in Portuguese West Africa* set forth details confirming the reports of Nevinson and others. In 1909 his firm began a boycott of São Tomé cocoa. In the same year Charles Swan, a missionary with experience in Angola, published an account of an inquiry into forced labor conditions in the interior of Angola. In 1913 the British Consul-General in West Africa visited Portuguese Guiné and confirmed that "slavery exists today in Portuguese Guiné, although it is, of course, carried on clandestinely." A year later John Harris presented a severe condemnation of contract labor in Angola, and in 1925 an American sociologist, Edward Alsworth Ross, visited Angola and Moçambique and submitted a report on labor abuses to the Temporary Slavery Commission of the League of Nations.

One of the most significant reports on native labor was presented by Henrique Galvão during a secret session of the Portuguese National Assembly in 1947. Galvão focused on the problem of widespread emigration and the resultant labor shortage which, he claimed, was a result of "the physical incapacity and decadence of the people, lack of medical care, undernourishment, a declining birth rate, infant mortality, and disabilities and deaths resulting from work . . ." In addition, he confirmed that mass dislocation of workers and existing working conditions had brought the colonies "frightful demographic impoverishment."

Galvão's denunciation of labor conditions was followed by a visit to Angola in 1954 by an Englishman, Basil Davidson, who in several articles and a book reported that the system of labor exploitation continued and that his inquiries "reaped overwhelming evidence of slavery in the same 'contract labor' form which Nevinson, Sir John Harris, and Ross describe." Two years later Marvin Harris, an anthropologist at Columbia University, visited Moçambique and in 1958 published a critique of labor conditions in the colony. There, according to revised conditions of the 1909 Transvaal-Moçambique Convention and the Portuguese-South African Convention of 1928, South Africa was permitted to recruit one hundred thousand laborers annually in Moçambique. In return Lourenço Marques was guaranteed a percentage of the Transvaal transit traffic. Harris criticized the high mortality rate among the African miners as well as the low wages. Analyzing the African's dilemma, he indicated that Portuguese policy decrees that those who cannot find employment in the carefully regulated labor markets of Moçambique's cities face the alternative of emigrating to the mines or being conscripted as *shibalos* or forced laborers.

Shortly after the outbreak of the Angolan war in 1961, Ghana accused Portugal of violating the Abolition of Forced Labour Convention. The complaint, however, contained numerous inaccuracies and was presented to the International Labour Organisation during a time when the Portuguese Overseas Ministry had initiated several reforms. An investigating commission therefore exonerated Portugal of many of Ghana's charges of improper labor practices. The commission noted a sharp reduction in the number of *shibalos* and commended the Portuguese government for its new labor legislation. The effectiveness of such legislation, however, was questioned by Harris in subsequent writings and by Moçambique nationalist reports which emanated from Dar er Salaam.

Factors other than slavery and forced labor characterized Portugal's difficulties in Africa. Not until the late nineteenth century were the scientific expeditions of Major Serpa Pinto and others undertaken in an attempt to fulfill the dream of uniting Angola and Moçambique, a dream that was shattered by the ambitious schemes of Cecil Rhodes. Nor did the Revolution of 1910 and the subsequent establishment of the Republic offer much hope for Portugal's imperial design, for, according to V. de Bragança-Cunha, at home the nation was "without economic activity, without capital and almost without men capable of carrying a movement of national reconstruction." Lacking resources and challenged by the ambitions of other nations, a languishing Portugal somehow managed to maintain its grip on the African colonies, attesting not only to the nation's fortitude but to its profound belief in its imperial and colonial destiny.

Colonial Policy

Present colonial policy echoes past policy, a fact that is supported by a historical review of policy formulation and implementation. Three general periods can be identified for analysis: (1) the discoveries, expansion, and colonization beginning in the fifteenth century; (2) the conquest and pacification of territories in Africa from as early as the sixteenth century well into the twentieth; and (3) the period of exaggerated misconceptions of Portuguese colonial destiny as manifested since 1926.

The outlines of colonial policy were clearly established during the early period of expansion and colonization. The political objective was to control Africa and other areas to build an empire based on friendly alliances. The economic objective was the dominance of international markets by controlling a network of key commercial centers. Another objective was the evangelization of uncivilized peoples and the instilling of European culture into the indigenous African cultural values.

From the beginnings of the discoveries, the Portuguese lacked manpower and financial resources to carry out a full-scale conquest and pacification of their empire. Not until the late nineteenth century, with the maneuvering for colonial possessions by European powers and the loss of territory claimed between Angola and Moçambique, did Portugal seriously turn its attention to Africa. Divided political elements were unified by a national consciousness that Portuguese Africa had not only to be defended but be occupied and developed. Once the frontiers of the African territories were determined by treaty, Portuguese soldiers and administrators attempted to pacify the warlike African tribes that for many centuries had resisted the Portuguese presence. So formidable was this task that the campaigns of pacification were not terminated until the mid-1930's. The period was marked by the emergence of a new generation of colonial administrators and policymakers whose views and writings in part reflected past colonial traditions, exploits, and valor, but also inspired the Portuguese to focus on African problems. The pragmatic António Ennes, a royal commissioner for Moçambique, initiated a period of revitalized colonial policy. Ennes defended the notion that authority be decentralized among the colonies, that each colony develop autonomous administrative procedures, that Portuguese peasant immigration be limited, that the African be obliged to submit to forced labor conditions, and that wherever possible Portuguese values be inculcated in native peoples. Under Ennes' leadership and that of his successors—Joaquim Mousinho de Albuquerque, Ayres d'Ornellas, Freire de Andrade, who served in Moçambique, and Henrique de Paiva Couceiro, Eduardo Ferreira da Costa, and José Norton de Matos, who became Angolan administrators—a flurry of reform and legislation was enacted. Decentralized administration and autonomy were perhaps these men's most important contributions to colonial policy. Otherwise, they reasserted principles of traditional policy: imperial consolidation through integration of scattered territories and exploitation of the African laborer. These men, with the exception perhaps of Norton de Matos, differed from Portuguese nineteenth century liberals who had insisted that native populations be granted legal status and protection as Portuguese citizens. Ennes and his contemporaries, however, did influence legislation which in 1921 was incorporated into a Native Assistance Code. By speaking Portuguese, remaining employed, and divesting himself of tribal customs, the African could under the Code attain *assimilado* or civilized status. Otherwise, he remained subject to and exploited by discriminating Portuguese law and rules.

Norton de Matos argued vigorously for a humanistic native policy to accompany the new administrative order. He criticized the prevailing contract labor conditions and urged his subordinates to proceed with the task of acculturation and the "unification of a single nation." Accordingly, there would be "no discrimination among regions, peoples, races, colors, and ideologies." The native policy would civilize and achieve a "perfect assimilation" of peoples throughout the colonies. His grandiose scheme was to be carried out slowly during a period of 150 years. Interestingly, Norton de Matos later became the presidential candidate of the political opposition to Salazar. He continued to advocate his earlier views, which, although fundamentally not much different from traditional and New State colonial philosophy, represented moderate criticism of Portugal's consistent failure to put into practice an enlightened and humanistic native policy.

The ideas of Ennes and his contemporaries provided the basis for New

State legislation which evolved with the promulgation of native statutes in 1926 and 1929, the Colonial Act of 1930, the Organic Charter of 1933 (modified in 1935 and 1945), and the Overseas Reform Act. The general principles of this legislation, which are incorporated into the Portuguese constitution, were set forth by Salazar, who served as Colonial Minister in 1930, and by his successor, Armindo Monteiro. These principles enabled the New State to reassert its imperial presence in Africa. Accordingly, the nation would "fulfill its historic mission of colonization in the lands of the discoveries." The overseas territories were called "provinces" and as such became integrally part of the nation. The New State centralized administration thereby countering the trend of the 1920's toward financial and political autonomy. As in the past, attention was focused on native policy, which continued to favor assimilation of the African through education into a position of integration within Portuguese society. According to Portuguese theoreticians like Joaquim da Silva Cunha, the policy of assimilation meant essentially that all inhabitants of the colonial territories, whether white or black and irrespective of their level of cultural development, must be regarded as equal in all respects and subject to the laws of the mother country. A policy of assimilation is founded on the "idea that there are no essential differences between races. In essence, all men are equal . . ." Another Portuguese writer, António Joaquim Alfaro Cardoso, describes native policy in terms realistically characteristic of Portuguese attitudes toward the African:

> This raw native has to be looked at as an adult with a child's mentality . . . He needs to be tutored . . . guided in the choice of the work suited to his abilities—in short, educated, physically, morally, and professionally . . . The practical result is that the educated natives consider themselves truly Portuguese . . . they are the first to manifest their patriotism.

In effect, the policy of assimilation served the Portuguese interest of maintaining the status quo and as such became so selective that it affected the legal status of less than one per cent of the African population.

Confronted by international controversy and pressures concerning colonial policy and by the reality that the professed policy of cultural integration had failed, the Salazar government all but abandoned its emphasis on assimilation in the 1950's. Instead, a transformation was to take place through the establishment and promotion of colonization projects in which Portuguese and Africans would participate. Large-scale immigration of white settlers was encouraged (there was a sixfold increase in the white population in Angola and Moçambique during the generation spanning the years 1930 and 1960), and the emergence of urban pockets of white settlers not only was contrary to but served to discredit the ideals of colonial legislation. At the same time the regime at last turned to economic development in the colonies. The government and the privileged Portuguese monopolies invested their capital in the extraction of petroleum, iron ore, and other raw materials, a process that was accompanied by a further exploitation of African labor.

The failure of the regime's early colonial legislation and the contradiction between assimilation and integration in theory and segregation and white minority rule in practice were reasons for the government's reevaluation of current policies. Furthermore, internal and international pressures were in evidence. On the one hand, disorder within all the colonies during the late 1950's prompted the government to strengthen security and armed forces there. The Angolan rebellion in 1961 was the African's culminating challenge to ineffectual Portuguese policy and also a turning point in history. On the other hand, the United Nations and other international organizations had begun to condemn Portuguese colonial practices.

Revision of old legislation was called for, and new reforms immediately were promulgated. The new measures were the creation of Adriano Moreira, who was appointed Overseas Minister in 1961. Essentially the new legislation reaffirmed Portugal's missionary role in Africa and attempted to provide administrative and economic decentralization. The decrees related to the establishment of municipal assemblies, commissions, and local committees; the functioning of municipal courts; the recognition of village councils as local administrative bodies; the establishment of provincial settlement boards; and the occupation and granting of land concessions.

Acknowledging the failure of its policy of assimilation, the government abolished the native statute, thereby giving the African populations "wider possibilities of looking after their interests and participating in the administration of their affairs." Finally, new legislation established measures to promote national economic integration. Beginning in 1962 "all barriers to the free movement of goods among the various national territories . . . will be abolished."

It is too early to assess these policy changes which, if put into practice, could provide the Salazar regime with an element of heretofore unknown flexibility. It is safe to assume, however, that these "token" reforms have had little impact upon the overseas territories. Administrative decentralization appeared to be minimal and meaningless under dictatorial order. Moreira presumably had emerged much too quickly as an important government figure and as a reformist who challenged the old order; he was abruptly replaced in late 1962. The native statute had shielded ineffectual practices, and there was little hope of increased African participation in politics; the former discriminatory restrictions remained in practice if not in theory. At the same time, relaxation of economic barriers contributed to colonial prosperity in the mid-1960's, particularly in Angola.

Few critics of the New State's colonial legislation can withstand the suppression of dictatorial rule. Three who have suggested policy modifications and who today remain critical of current developments are Francisco Pinto da Cunha Leal, Manuel José Homen de Mello, and Pacheco de Amorim.

Cunha Leal, a former Minister of Finance under the Republic, has been a consistent critic of Salazar's policies. In his book, written in 1930, *Oliveira Salazar, filomeno da Câmara,* Cunha Leal attacked the policies of then Colonial Minister Salazar and in particular the Colonial Act of 1930. Cunha Leal argued that Salazar's "designation of 'Portuguese Colonial Empire' is unsuitable and pretentious, and the idea of forcibly halting colonial deficits is ridiculous." He continued his criticism of Salazar in *A pátria em perigo* and other books published in the 1960's. Essentially Cunha Leal advocated granting self-determination to the overseas territories yet linking the territories to the metropole in a federation of states.

A similar position, more precisely spelled out, was taken by Manuel José Homem de Mello, a former deputy in Salazar's National Assembly. Writing in *Portugal, o ultramar e o futuro,* Homem de Mello called for structural changes that would permit Portugal to preserve its influence in the overseas territories. Portugal, he argued, should prepare the territories for eventual autonomy by establishing regional assemblies, increasing educational programs to eliminate illiteracy, promoting free trade unions and cooperative movements and other reforms.

The thesis of Homem de Mello and Cunha Leal was rebutted by Pacheco de Amorim, who in *Tres caminhos* also argued that official colonial policy of "tendential integration" was based on ideas initiated by António Ennes and continued during the Republic; that such policy affirmed in theory but not in practice that Portugal and the overseas territories would eventually establish one "pluricultural and pluricontinental Nation"; and that this "association discredits the thesis of unity." Pacheco de Amorim favored "authentic integration or assimilation" that would centralize Portugal and the territories into a united nation. A commitment to united nationhood under common legislation, government, and administration would accompany a process of administrative decentralization within each territory, he argued.

Difficult as it may be to differentiate among these various positions, the views of Salazar, Cunha Leal, Homem de Mello, and Pacheco de Amorim similarly reflect one traditional colonial tendency: all profess faith in the dream of a Lusitanian community; all view the African territories as the key to maintenance of the empire; all fail to recognize immediate independence for the territories.

TWO

INSTITUTIONAL FORCES AND CHANGE

The failure of Portuguese policies to meet their objectives may be attributed partially to structural difficulties and deficiencies in the political, economic, social, and cultural matrix of Portugal itself. This matrix incorporates institutional forces that serve as the supports and countersupports to authoritarian order. An examination of these forces reveals consensual links, tension, and conflict between the metropole and the overseas territories as well as alternatives for Portuguese Africa that are largely dependent on changes of existing conditions in Portugal.

Structural Problems

Structural weaknesses and rigid control of Portuguese political, economic, social, and cultural life are directly tied to the ineffectiveness of colonial policy. Intransigent political leaders and a powerful aristocratic elite have sustained four decades of dictatorial order through their resistance to social change and an inability to resolve many basic internal and external problems that face underdeveloped nations in general.

Suppression is the manifestation of the political order. The dictatorship came to power in response to the tragic and chaotic republican experiment that witnessed the rise and fall of 44 governments between 1910 and 1926. Although backed by the armed forces, the Roman Catholic Church, and the wealthy aristocracy, Prime Minister António de Oliveira Salazar could not guarantee a viable political order at home and in the colonies. The so-called stability of the New State was marred by riots during 1931 in Madeira, Portuguese Guiné, and the Açores. A 1936 revolt by two naval ships failed; military uprisings collapsed in 1946, 1947, 1952, 1959, 1961, and in early 1962. African nationalists initiated revolts in Angola during 1961, in Guiné during 1962, and in Moçambique during 1964. The African revolts became guerrilla struggles, necessitating that Portugal maintain one hundred thousand Portuguese troops overseas.

The firm rule of Salazar and his conservative, sometimes fascist supporters replaced the liberal oligarchy that permeated Portuguese politics during the late nineteenth and early twentieth centuries. The divisions which racked the first republic—landowners versus peasants, labor versus capital, Church versus anti-clericals, and the like—continued to persist although peasants, workers, anti-clericals, and others who opposed the dictatorship were effectively suppressed. Salazar ruled as a "monarch" and achieved his "reforms" by maintaining his disbelief in democracy, universal suffrage, and equality. Always a believer in "hierarchy," he established his 1933 constitution, inspired by the *Rerum Novarum* of Pope Leo XIII and the *Quadragessimo Anno* of Pius XI. His "unitary and corporate state" consisted of a two-chamber parliament: the National Assembly and the Corporative Chamber. Of the 130 deputies (opposition candidates have yet to be elected) in the National Assembly, which meets twice annually to recommend, not approve, legislation, Angola and Moçambique are each represented by seven deputies, the Cape Verde archipelago by two, Portuguese Guiné by one, and São Tomé and Príncipe by one. Little is reported of the Corporative Chamber's activities; not until 1958 was legislation enacted creating the first eight corporations. Also part of the system, the União Nacional was designed to unite all political groups into what is not a one-party state, but a state without parties.

By winning a fourth of the votes in the 1958 presidential elections the generally weak and divided opposition, led by General Humberto Delgado, seriously challenged the dictatorship and marked a turning point in Portuguese politics. The government's reaction to the 1958 experience was to abolish direct suffrage in presidential elections (the President is chosen by an electoral college consisting of members of the National Assembly and the Corporative Chamber as well as municipal officials). This, plus the Angola outbreak in 1961 and the loss of Goa at the end of the year, encouraged discontented students to demonstrate each year thereafter. From the student movement emerged a new opposition leadership, Christian Democrat and Socialist in outlook, which focused its attention on the necessity for solutions to basic issues at home and abroad.

The students and other Portuguese were dissatisfied with the results of the regime. One of the many unresolved problems was the question of who would succeed Salazar. The independent newspaper *O Diário de Lisboa* once commented: "Regimes based on the authority and prestige of a single man run the risk of a break in administrative continuity the day the man disappears from the political scene." The official *Diário da Manhã* retorted that Portugal had avoided the danger of placing power in the hands of a single man. (The President, who is elected every seven years, appoints the Premier. Although Premier Salazar has never been replaced, there was an abortive attempt to persuade the President to exercise his authority in April 1961.)

As Minister of Finance in 1928, Salazar assumed control over governmental receipts and expenditures and, two years later, over all government activity. Although successful in balancing the budget and stemming inflation, he faced then, as now, many problems that have undermined economic development: low income, underdevelopment, weak industrial base, poor natural resources, and the like. To resolve these problems he established his corporative structure, each corporation being a legal entity composed of employer and employee associations engaged in the same or affiliated class of economic, social, or professional activity. The "corporative state" has had little impact on economic life, although it has been the focus of many studies by New State theorists.

More important than attempts to constitute a corporate state have been several economic planning schemes. The First Development Plan (1953-1958) followed administrative reorganization under the Law of Economic Reconstruction (1935-1950) and aimed "to raise the standard of life and to create new jobs both in European Portugal and overseas." The plan's primary objective was to establish infrastructure for development by large-scale government investments in communications, transport, agriculture, and industry. The objectives of the Second Development Plan (1959-1964) were to accelerate the growth rate of gross national product, improve living standards, solve unemployment problems, and improve Portugal's balance of payments situation. In the overseas territories the plan was to draw up an inventory of available resources, develop infrastructure in transport, agricultural irrigation, and electrical power, and promote colonization schemes. Angola was allocated roughly half of the overseas budget and Moçambique about a third. To follow the Second Development Plan the government launched an interim plan for 1965-1967 (a Third Development Plan would be established thereafter). The plan called for a $1,700 million investment of which forty per cent would go to the overseas territories; under the plan, the annual economic growth rate would increase from 4.5 to 6.5 per cent.

Accompanying the development plans was the liberalization of foreign trade patterns, a departure from an introverted financial policy and aversion to foreign loans and credits, and increased economic integration evidenced by Portugal's joining the Organisation for Economic Cooperation and Development (OECD), the European Free Trade Association, the International Monetary Fund, the World Bank, and the General Agreement on Tariffs and Trade. In Lisbon the Banco de Fomento Nacional was founded with the purpose of financing and guiding economic expansion in metropolitan Portugal and the overseas territories. In 1962 a "single market" free trade area was established between Portugal and the overseas dependencies. Tariffs were to be reduced and eventually abolished over a ten-year period.

Recent economic development and expansion resulted in some accomplishments for the regime, including the establishment of the first integrated iron and steel industry at Seixal near Lisbon, an atomic reactor, the Douro River Hydroelectric project, a large chemical manufacturing plant, several automobile assembly plants, the Tagus river bridge, and a large new shipyard. At the same time the construction industry reached record production, spurred by the arrival of tourists needing houses and hotels. In the overseas provinces, lack of capital, inadequate transport facilities, and a scarcity of skilled industrial workers were obstacles to rapid economic development. However, large quantities of raw materials were exploited to support manufacturing in the metropole. In Angola, the most valuable of the territories, resources were practically untapped, with the exception of the coffee, diamond, oil, and iron ore industries which had expanded substantially in recent years.

The "liberal" colonial policies and increased economic investment and production coincided with the challenge of the emerging national liberation movements. Portugal's intent was to strengthen its hold on the territories by encouraging foreign investment. Mining concessions and legislation permitting large-scale foreign investment allowed the exploitation of considerable mineral wealth, including, in Angola, diamonds, iron ore, petroleum, bauxite, and manganese and, in Moçambique, coal, beryllium, and other minerals. As a result, foreign or partially foreign-owned companies held exclusive rights to prospect for minerals and exploit large tracts of land. The Angola Diamond Company held exclusive rights over more than one million square kilometers, Petrangol controlled petroleum rights over large areas in Angola and the U.S.-owned Cabinda Gulf Company over part of Cabinda, and German and Danish capital combined with Portuguese interests to exploit the largest iron ore deposits. In Moçambique, Belgium and Portuguese interests controlled a concession over coal deposits of four hundred million tons, and two U.S.-owned firms exercised exclusive petroleum rights over a large area. Evident also was the growing financial interests in the Portuguese African territories by South African firms, particularly the Anglo-American Corporation and its subsidiary De-Beers Corporation.

This foreign activity, according to a report issued in 1965 by the United Nations' committee investigating colonial countries and peoples, resulted in "a system of mutual benefits," whereby the government provided mining companies with cheap labor, tax exemptions, and other concessions. At the same time contributions, revenues, and loans made available to the government by the companies assisted Portugal to continue its control over its territories and "to finance its repressive measures and military operations against the African inhabitants." The United Nations report concluded that under the colonial system Africans were deprived of their sovereign rights over the natural resources: "The great majority of the peasants have thus been forced to become tenant farmers of the European landowners or foreign companies. The conditions under which they live are reminiscent of serfdom." According to the report, foreign capital dominated all sectors of economic life, "fostering exploitation of the basic resources without regard to balanced economic development, and reinforcing Portuguese policy which denies the peoples of the territories their rightful participation in the economic and political life."

These conditions reflected the very serious economic problems that challenged the dictatorial order at home and overseas. Traditionally a shortage of capital plagued the present regime and other regimes dating back to the sixteenth century. Desirous of preserving self-interests, many Portuguese investors hesitated to contribute to development schemes, and as a result capital and the economy remained controlled by an influential clique of industrialists and landowners who in turn were closely tied to, and allegedly controlled by, foreign capital. (Foreigners invested substantial capital in Portuguese enterprise during the 1960's.) Among the industrialists were prominent families directly and indirectly associated with many sectors of the economy: the Pinto Basto family, prominent in shipping, for example; the Espírito Santo family, associated with a bank chain and luxury hotels; the Pinto de Azevedo family, which controlled the textile industry, two prominent daily newspapers, cork and insurance enterprise, and large colonial plantations; and the De Mello family which dominated the Companhia União Fabril, a holding company that controlled some banks, iron and steel, cement, and other related industries at home and abroad.

These and a handful of other families comprise an industrial aristocracy that closely cooperates with an upper-middle-class elite of entrepreneurs and privileged officials and former officials (ministers, ambassadors, governors, etc.) of the New State regime. The two groups work together to control the boards of directors of the nation's largest enterprises and such important banks as the Banco Nacional Ultramarino, Banco Português Atlântico, Banco Burnay, Banco Espírito Santo, and Banco Borges e Irmão. Despite interlocking of the industrial elites and the New State, the tie between domestic and foreign capital has been such that European-oriented industrialists pressure the system to move toward economic integration with Europe. This fact plus the necessity for foreign credits and loans (to offset the estimated more than $100 million expenditures for the military defense of the African territories as well as Portugal's annual trade deficits, caused by increasing demand for war armaments, foodstuffs, textile raw materials, and machinery and equipment) accounted in part for the changes that brought about the regime's break with introverted financial policy.

A few landowners constitute part of the influential Portuguese elite. Official statistics show that some three thousand farms occupy nearly forty per cent of all arable land and that the estates of the Duke of Palmela, the Duke of Cadaval, Posser de Andrade, and Santos Jorge comprise 95,000 hectares. In contrast, about half of the 800,000 farms occupy one hectare or less. This discrepancy between the few large and many small landholders is particularly significant, since 45 per cent of Portugal's active labor force is engaged in the agricultural sector and contributes little more than a fifth to the gross domestic product.

The industrial and agrarian elites thus exert considerable influence on the Portuguese economy and contribute to the intransigence of dictatorial order. The resistance of these elites to change is directly attributable to shortages of capital and labor, ineffective civil administration, and economic and financial instability. In recent years nonagricultural output has been slowed by anti-inflation measures deemed necessary because of considerable military expenditure (40 to 45 per cent of the national budget). Furthermore, to support the war effort, luxury taxes on consumer goods brought disastrous results to small businessmen and to lower income families. In its 1964 survey, the OECD warned that the vast needs for economic development were undermined by the war effort. Emphasis was needed on investment and manufacturing, and a number of financial reforms were called for. Furthermore, according to the report, public initiative was needed for carrying out important investment and reform measures in agriculture where the high cost of living, low productivity, and underemployment resulted in a labor shortage caused by heavy legal and illegal emigration to France, Germany, and other countries.

A leading Portuguese economist and former Minister of the Economy, Luiz Teixeira Pinto, states in his *Alguns aspectos da teoria do crescimento económico* that the economy suffered from "immobility . . . unparalleled in other countries." He characterized Portuguese development as beset by low incomes, unemployment, low diversification of production and export, and a low level of technical accomplishment. As Minister of the Economy he later advocated agrarian reform and structural changes in the agricultural sector. The significance of such criticism, however, is difficult to assess since Teixeira Pinto no longer serves as Minister and much of the economy, particularly the agricultural sector, remains stagnated by low productivity, ill-conceived attempts at modernization, and improper planning.

A rigid social stratification characterizes Portuguese society. Per capita national income of roughly $300 remains one of the lowest in Europe, and income on the farms is perhaps two-thirds of that figure. Furthermore, income is unevenly distributed. Urban workers and rural farm laborers suffer from low wages and underemployment while at the same time not being allowed to organize protests against the regime. Income inequalities are evident in the tax structure: indirect taxes represent more than forty per cent of budget income, whereas income taxes do not greatly affect the wealthy elite.

A similar but more complex social pattern exists in the African territories where a white minority elite of civil and military administrators, entrepreneurs, and large landholders shares values common to the metropolitan elite. This colonial elite is distinguished from the two or three hundred thousand white settlers who are of the lower middle and working class but who in turn represent a social stratum above that of the majority of Africans. Traditionally the Portuguese have favored the mulatto over the black or "native" African. The "assimilated" African often was placed in lower level administrative positions. Having thus achieved recognition and status within the Portuguese social system, these privileged Africans actually wielded great authority and power over the native African population. The Portuguese demonstrated much success by appointing loyal black Africans as district officers (*chefes de posto*) and in "buying off" many of the petty chiefs. The effect was not, as many critics have suggested, to undermine the authority of the petty chiefs. Indeed Portuguese policy served to strengthen local authority and to assure the continuance of political apathy among Africans and of a native economy based on shifting cultivation. One tends to agree with the view of the economic historian, Richard Hammond, that the Portuguese governmental ma- chinery does not rigidly control the daily life of the natives with the objec- tive of keeping them in ignorance and isolation. It may be, as Hammond contends, that such a policy is not deliberately contrived and executed. Nevertheless, the facts verify that Portuguese policymakers have demon- strated little or no concern for education of the illiterate African masses or for integrating them into colonial society.

At home and in overseas Africa, according to official statistics and information in the early 1960's, Portugal lagged behind the welfare pro- grams established in other European countries: health insurance and benefits, old age compensation, unemployment insurance, and the like. In relation to population, hospitals, infirmaries and other health facilities, doctors and nurses, and services and assistance, especially in Africa, were badly deficient. Sickness subsidies were available only to workers who had contributed to social welfare funds for a lengthy period of time and were calculated in proportion to salaries, thereby excluding or limiting assistance to Portuguese and Africans alike. Very minimal assistance for the aged was available to industrial workers at the age of 65 (in general, farm labor- ers were not covered by this provision). Apparently no compensation was available to unemployed workers. Mortality rates for those with infectious diseases and for infants were high in Portugal—among the highest in Europe. These and other indicators support the view of many observers that social life and institutions have not been a major concern of dicta- torial rule in Portugal and the African territories.

Cultural censorship also has characterized Portuguese rule, resulting in the decline of an intelligentsia which long ago lost its vitality and political effectiveness. Cultural life was affected by faculty purges at the University of Lisbon in 1935, 1946, 1947, and 1962 and by the arrest and imprison- ment of hundreds of demonstrating students during recent years. Controls on mass media were enforced (newspapers insert the note "Visado pela Commissão Censura"). Drawing attention to an apparent need to conceal truth, in 1963 Salazar defended his regime's censorship as "the elimination of that which may tend to warp public opinion and to harm the superior interests of the nation." This attitude was challenged publicly a year later by Bishop Eurico Dias Nogueira who stated: "On the day when the press places itself at the service of a political regime . . . it ceases to . . . serve the truth."

In May 1965 the government banned the Portuguese Society of Writers, which had awarded its Grand Fiction Prize to an Angolan, Luandino Vieira, who had been condemned as a criminal for alleged "terrorist activities in Angola." Previously the Society had nominated novelist Aquilino Ribeiro for the Nobel Prize at a time when he was arrested for the publication of a book critical of conditions in Portugal. In September 1965 the Casa dos Estudantes do Império in Lisbon, considered a "center of subversion" for students from the colonies, was closed.

A thread of cultural opposition has outlasted the Salazar dictatorship, however, and is represented by the literary magazine, *Seara Nova*, founded in 1921. Linked to the ideas of such important social writers of the nineteenth century as Antero de Quental, Eça de Queiroz, and Oliveira Martins, it favors the education of an intellectual elite and the improvement of Portugal's political culture. Although now led by a new generation of intellectuals, many of whom have been arrested frequently or forced into exile, this magazine has not filled the cultural gap left by the dictatorship, a cultural gap characterized by an insignificant contemporary literature, by a lack of originality in the fine arts, and by deficient historical scholarship of the twentieth century.

In the 1930's Salazar stated: "We have developed a sham culture . . . we have brought up a nation's mentality to be passive instead of active." The "sham" culture would be overcome through insistence on order, he claimed: "It is from the authoritarian states that art can expect something . . . Beauty and order are inseparable." To maintain that "order," however, the government allocated large percentages of its budget to the military and police and only small amounts to education and cultural activities. According to the 1950 census, illiteracy was 40 per cent, although recent unofficial claims place the figure at 20 per cent. Nevertheless, school attendance is low, and only a small percentage of school children advance beyond primary school. In fact, Portugal lags behind most other European nations in educational achievement; official statistical data reveal that Portugal is deficient in public spending for education, school construction, and enforcement of extensive compulsory education. The government's cultural activities are directed by the Secretariado Nacional da Informação, which issues propagandistic pamphlets and books; arranges expositions of art, drama presentations, occasional musical concerts and ballet; administers a museum of popular art; directs the national radio broadcasting system; and awards annual prizes for literature, the arts, and cinema.

In the African territories educational policy allows natives to assimilate into Portuguese life, but it has failed to provide any real opportunity for the native to meet rigid educational requirements. In reality, education for the African masses has been almost totally ignored, as attested by a literacy rate of no more than one or two per cent. The educated African might threaten Portuguese political interests, a view frequently advanced by Portuguese officials who argue that natives should acquire "an appropriate social background" before being educated.

Within the overseas territories there are various levels and types of education. In the urban or more populated areas, government, private, and mission schools offer a four-year primary level course. In "indigenous" or rural regions church missions and the government offer African children a "rudimentary" course of instruction of from three to five years. Secondary education is available in a limited number of schools in the African territories and is open to those who pass state examinations. No university exists in the African territories, although courses are offered by the Estudos Gerais Universitários de Angola e de Moçambique, which is supervised by the Ministry of Education in Angola and Moçambique. It is evident from official figures on numbers of schools, attendance, etc., that church and state have failed to build an educational system that serves more than a small percentage of the African population.

The regime has attempted to cultivate a colonial literature with varying degrees of success. The number of Portuguese periodicals dedicated to colonial matters is ample, but few significant literary works have been produced in overseas Africa. The Overseas Ministry offers prizes, but colonial literature has been restricted by the small numbers of educated Africans and the difficulty of obtaining publication in Portugal for original literary works. Viriato da Cruz and other Angolans attempted to establish a journal, A Mensagem, which was banned after its second issue. Two Angolans, Mário de Andrade and Agostinho Neto, have achieved notoriety as African poets. Neto, however, was arrested as a subversive in 1960. Eventually Neto, Andrade, Cruz, and most other important African literary figures found their way to exile and assumed leadership of nationalist organizations. There is evidence of an indigenous Cape Verdean literature, and a number of Portuguese writers have cultivated colonial themes with moderate success, but no purely Portuguese African literature has fully developed under colonial rule.

Supports and Countersupports

The structural difficulties and problems of the Salazar regime are evidence of rigidity and immobility in the colonies as well as in the Portuguese political system itself. In order to understand the relationship of the dictatorship to the African territories it is useful to examine the important political forces that play a major role in shaping the policies of continuity and those that from time to time manifest their dissatisfaction with the current stalemate. Among the former are the props of the regime: the military and police, the bureaucracy, the oligarchy, and the Church. Among the dissatisfied forces are ostracized elements: the opposition parties, part of the intelligentsia and the students, urban labor, and the rural manual field laborer.

Salazar was ushered into power by the armed forces which, together with several police organizations, continue to give him essential support. The main source of the regime's strength rests with the widely feared secret political Polícia Internacional e de Defesa do Estado (PIDE), which is modeled on the German Gestapo. Its leadership was trained by the Gestapo in the 1930's and by Italians sent to Portugal by Mussolini during the Spanish Civil War. It is this writer's belief that the "fascist" leanings attributed to the New State regime emanate principally from the PIDE and remnants of the other police and military organizations. The PIDE has established an elaborate informer system that operates efficiently throughout Portugal and less effectively in the African territories. Under New State legislation any person can be imprisoned without charge for three months, a period that can be extended to six months with permission of the Minister of the Interior. Habeas corpus is denied detainees, and the political opposition has carefully documented hundreds of cases of torture and assassination as well as the abuse of political prisoners in the isolated "concentration camp" of Tarrafel on the Cape Verde island of Santiago.

Within this police state the PIDE functions autonomously yet works closely with the military, its director usually being an army officer. The military, particularly the army, exercises extensive control over other police organizations, which also cooperate closely with the PIDE. Among these organizations is the grey-uniformed "civil" Polícia de Segurança Pública (PSP) utilized daily in urban areas and occasionally for preliminary clashes with political demonstrators. In contrast, the Guarda Nacional Republicana (GNR), established under the Republic to deal with counterrevolutions, functions mainly in rural areas. Its heavily armed 6,000-man force deals with strikes and demonstrations. Although both the PSP and GNR are attached to the Ministry of the Interior, they are commanded by military officers and armed with truncheons, grenades, machine guns, and armored cars. The green-shirted Legião Portuguesa is a paramilitary organization of possibly sixty thousand volunteers and fanatical supporters of the regime who in their spare time drill under retired army and naval officers. Rounding out the police organization are the customs officials or Guarda Fiscal and the criminal investigators known as the Polícia Judiciária.

The army, which absorbs ninety per cent of the military budget, is the most important of the armed forces. In spite of its being a major bulwark of support for the regime, it is beset by internal division. High-ranking career officers, drawn from or closely associated with the elites, are sharply differentiated from the lowly paid Portuguese and African conscripts. The native African, socialized to some extent by his military service, nevertheless cannot be trusted by his superiors, and defections are not uncommon. Attempted coups against the regime, however, have been launched by officers for personal, ideological, or humanistic reasons. Abortive revolts or plots were staged by fifty junior officers on October 10, 1946; by army officers in April 1947; by thirty noncommissioned officers conspiring on behalf of the monarchy and rallying around the Defense Minister Fernando Santos Costa in August 1958; by seven officers and sixteen civilians in March 1959; by Defense Minister Júlio Botelho Moniz, who was dismissed from his post on April 13, 1961, after he and other military leaders issued an ultimatum demanding Salazar's resignation; and by Captain João Varela Gomes and army officers who attacked the Beja army barracks on January 1, 1962. Two major currents, one conservative and the other liberal, have characterized the division in the army. Santos Costa, a monarchist, a Catholic, and an ultraconservative, has represented one tendency. Sometimes identified as the "grey eminence" behind the regime he is a possible successor to Salazar. Botelho Moniz and, until his death in 1964, former President (1951-1958) Marshal Francisco Higino Craveiro Lopes have represented "liberals" in the army ranks who desire an end to colonial conflict and problems. Occasionally military figures assigned to administrative duty in Africa become too "Angolan" or "Moçambican" in their sentiments and are dismissed from their post. A case in point was the removal from office in 1962 of the Angolan governor general, Augusto Venâncio Deslandes. There was also the unexplained departure from Moçambique of Admiral Sarmento Rodrigues a few weeks before an official presidential visit.

The navy and air force are less important than the army but exercise some influence in Portuguese life, as exemplified by the aborted mutinies of October 1919 and September 1936 and the selection by the opposition of presidential candidates, Admiral Quintâo Meireles in 1951 and Air Force General Humberto Delgado in 1958. The 9,000-man navy's prestige is enhanced by the location in Lisbon of the naval headquarters of the North

Atlantic Treaty Organization. Additionally, an admiral, Américo Tomás, became President in 1958 and 1965.

The regime's mobilization of the bureaucratic machinery assures institutionalized support. Order, discipline, and subservience to the regime characterize the bureaucracy. The bureaucratic machinery encompasses the executive, legislative, and judicial branches of government, including the ministries, the National Assembly, and the Chamber of Corporations, the União Nacional, and related political, economic, and social agencies. Technically the bureaucracy is linked to the corporative system for which the basis is "the family and the moral and economic corporations." Accordingly, centralized executive authority working through the bureaucracy "leads the citizens to mutual understanding." However, executive power rests with the president of the Council of Ministers (Salazar), who is responsible neither to the legislative chambers nor to any other governmental agency.

Authority to administer colonial matters emanates from the Council of Ministers and filters through the Overseas Ministry. The Council may legislate decrees for the overseas territories and appoint and dismiss administrative officials. Though the Overseas Ministry is a permanent consultative body, the Overseas Council and several temporary consultative organizations convene infrequently to discuss general policy. Provincial authority is granted to governors general, district authority to governors, and local authority to administrators in conselhos or councils, circunscrições or circumscriptions, freguesias or parishes, postos or posts, and regedorias or village councils. Provincial legislative councils, through which local demands may be manifested, discuss and suggest policy matters. To fill these positions, particularly at higher echelons, an administrative elite of overseas career officials is trained in the Instituto Superior de Ciências Sociais e Política Ultramarina. High military officials, however, customarily occupy the posts of governor general and district governor. It is also true that metropolitan Portuguese predominate at the upper levels of the colonial service. Occasionally a black African assumes a position of importance, and Cape Verdeans frequently are placed at lower echelon positions. The hierarchical bureaucracy, with authority centralized in Lisbon but channeled to various administrative levels in the provinces, tends to restrict local initiative. The effect, argues James Duffy, is to discourage colonial development; furthermore, the failure to delegate specific authority results in a Portuguese tendency to rely on legislation and reports rather than on responsible administrative action.

The Roman Catholic Church has consistently supported the New State,

47377

although liberal dissenters frequently express dissatisfaction with governmental action and policy. Technically, Church and state have been divided since 1910 when politics abruptly shifted from monarchical to republican rule, the Jesuits were expelled, and Church property confiscated. The New State regime maintained the separation, but the constitution of 1933 conceded that diplomatic relations would be established between Portugal and the Vatican. The constitution itself was claimed to be modeled after the Papal encyclicals *Rerum Novarum* of Pope Leo XIII and *Quadragessimo Anno* of Pius XI. According to the 1940 concordat, the Church and state reconciled many of their differences, although there was no compensation for earlier confiscated property. This rapprochement and the Church's continued allegiance and support for the government are assured by a conservative Catholic majority led by Cardinal Patriarch Manuel Gonçalves Cerejeira, close friend and fellow member with Salazar of the now defunct Centro Católico party. In fact, the regime recruits many cabinet ministers and other officials from the conservative Catholic Centro Acadêmico da Democracia Cristã (CADC) in Coimbra. Associated with conservative Catholics is the secular group, the Opus Dei, which is slowly infiltrating Portuguese economic, social, and cultural life but has not permeated politics to the extent that it has in Spain. It has small influence in the universities, publishes at least one important cultural review, and controls several banks and commercial firms.

Although the Church hierarchy supports the regime, liberal Catholics frequently vent their criticism. In 1958 the Bishop of Oporto, António Ferreira Gomes (presently exiled in Spain) criticized worker's conditions in Portugal: "The Portuguese corporative state [has become] in reality the means of despoiling the Portuguese worker . . . Rags and tatters, hunger and misery are still widespread in Portugal." The Bishop's protest awakened many Catholics to side with the worker masses against the regime. Many of the priests of the Oporto diocese supported their bishop's position, and throughout the country, particularly in Lisbon, many priests expressed dissatisfaction with the regime. After 1958, dissenting Catholic priests and laymen rejected the notion of founding a Christian Democrat party and prudently worked through the Acção Católica and two of its youth branches, the Juventude Universitária Católica (JUC) and the Juventude Obrera Católica (JOC). In the late 1950's the government closed *O Trabalhador*, organ of the JOC, for its "subversive" criticism of worker's conditions. In 1962 and thereafter a progressive movement emerged from the ranks of the Catholic youth. The original demands for university reforms quickly spread to protests directed at the regime itself. During the 1965 electoral campaign Catholic laymen, many of them sons and nephews of prominent figures in the regime, signed anti-Salazar manifestoes demanding liberal reforms at home and autonomy for the colonies. All this activity appeared to foreshadow the emergence of a potentially important Christian democratic or socialist movement opposed to the Church hierarchy and the Salazar regime.

Although, according to the Missionary Agreement of 1940 and the Missionary Statute of 1941, Portuguese missions are subsidized by the government and guaranteed free exercise of authority, the Church is weakened by its failure to allocate sufficient manpower and financial resources to the African territories. Furthermore, a large percentage of the African population is either animist or Muslim. Foreign Protestant missionaries have been influential, although overall Christian impact has not been substantial. In Guiné, for example, census data of 1950 revealed that Catholics and Protestants together represented less than one per cent of the "uncivilized population" of a half million inhabitants while in Moçambique there were roughly 350,000 Catholics and 100,000 Protestants in a population of 5.5 million. In contrast, 1.5 million Catholics and a half million Protestants constituted part of Angola's population of four million in 1950.

The Catholic hierarchy in Africa has criticized Portuguese colonial policy. In 1961 the Angolan hierarchy protested the arrests of Monsignor Manuel Mendes das Neves, the respected Vicar General of Luanda, and many other priests. In Moçambique, the Bishop of Beira, Sebastião Soares de Resende, who is the author of several books and publisher of the "liberal" newspaper Diário de Moçambique, has concerned himself with the exploitation and plight of the African worker.

Protestant missionaries have bitterly criticized the overseas administration and the Catholic Church for lagging in the insurmountable task of educating the poor, illiterate African masses. After the Angolan outbreak in 1961, the government and Catholic Church charged Protestant missionaries with subversion and political agitation, resulting in the exit from Angola of hundreds of missionaries, the death or imprisonment of many ministers and pastors, and the closing of many missions situated in the northern rebel-controlled region.

A small, wealthy group of entrepreneurs whose support for the regime has been rewarded with key concessions allowing for consolidation of economic power represents an oligarchy of perhaps not more than eleven families that control most of the nation's domestic and overseas industry. This group's hold on the economy has been tightened somewhat by rapidly expanding coffee, iron ore, and petroleum production in Angola. Although there is little evidence of its displeasure with New State policy, certain anxiety over the question of a successor to the aging Salazar and the fact that its hegemony is challenged to some extent by emergent "liberal" entrepreneurs oriented toward European markets and economic integration make this oligarchy at least a potential threat to the system it has supported for so many years.

Monarchist aspirations are evident among Salazar supporters in the military, Church, and oligarchy. An estimated twenty thousand monarchists back the pretender to the crown, Dom Duarte Nuno, Duke of Bragança and a descendant of the "conservative" line of Dom Miguel, who reigned briefly during a period dominated by civil war. Miguel's brother Pedro, first emperor of Brazil, succeeded in restoring the crown to his daughter Maria, the rightful heiress, and Miguel fled to exile in 1834. After the death of the last Portuguese king, Dom Manuel, in England in 1932, monarchists recognized the claim of the Miguelista line. Following the revocation in 1950 of the law preventing members of the royal house from living in Portugal, Duarte Nuno returned from Switzerland to reside in Portugal. He was supported by the Causa Monárquica, a monarchist organization officially recognized by the Salazar regime. General José Esquivel, a staunch supporter of the regime and close friend of Santos Costa, directs the Causa Monárquica, which has established a network of advisory committees through Portugal and the overseas territories. Its professed aim is to preserve the nation, restore the monarchy, and combat Communism. Its views are disseminated through pamphlets, manifestoes, the newspaper A Voz, and several magazines, including the literary journal *Tempo Presente*. The failure of many Portuguese to recognize Duarte Nuno as a logical successor to Salazar prompted one monarchist faction, led by Jacinto Ferreira and grouped around the weekly O *Debate*, to defect to the opposition, where it has been outspokenly critical of the Salazar regime. Also opposed to the Causa Monárquica and the regime is Princess Maria Pia de Saxe-Cobourg, the Duchess of Bragança, daughter of King Carlos and Manuelista claimant to the throne. Upon returning from exile in early 1965 she was immediately expelled by the Portuguese police, who accused her of complicity with the exiled opposition. The Princess is, in fact, associated with the "constitutional" and "independent" monarchists who back the opposition's Directório Democrata Social in Portugal and the Frente Patriótica de Libertação Nacional (FPLN) in exile.

Among elements ostracized by the regime, the political opposition at home and abroad represents a moderate challenge. Because political parties and movements are not tolerated, the opposition has remained generally weak and disorganized. Since the electoral campaign of General Delgado in 1958 and the split with the Seara Nova group of socialists, the Directório Democrata Social has loosely coalesced much of the domestic opposition composed of some military figures, independent Catholics, dissident monarchists, liberals, and old-guard republicans like Cunha Leal. Allowed to campaign during elections and to issue occasional manifestoes, this group's objective has been to effect political change through peaceful means, moderate demands, and negotiations with the government. An important opposition manifesto, published in 1961 and entitled "Program for the Democratization of the Republic," summed up opposition proposals of past years, its thirteen parts including demands for restoration of basic freedoms, cessation of the corporative organization, modification of administrative, juridical, educational and labor organization, and revision of overseas policy.

In 1962 Portuguese exiles founded the FPLN in Algiers and a year later chose General Delgado as its president. The FPLN attempted to coordinate its activities with the internal opposition and represent a loose coalition of individual liberals, socialists, Catholics, monarchists, and the Communist Party. In mid-1964 a small pro-Peking faction split from the Communist Party and established itself as the Frente de Acção Popular which supported a militant policy against the regime, a policy also supported by Delgado, who subsequently was not reelected president of the FPLN at its third congress. Delgado then formed a rival Frente Portuguesa de Libertação Nacional, which he headed until his mysterious assassination in early 1965.

Today the original FPLN remains in practice a popular front dominated by the Communist Party. Officially the FPLN's executive committee is comprised of one representative each from: the Communist Party, established in 1921, pro-Soviet and certainly the best organized of the opposition movements; the Movimento de Acção Revolucionária, a non-Communist left movement established in mid-1962 as an outgrowth of student unrest within Portugal; and the Movimento de Resistência Republicana, which is led by Cunha Leal and other oppositionists who lead the Directório Democrata Social within Portugal. Three independents—Manuel Sertório, Piteiro Santos, and José María Ervedosa—also serve on the executive committee. Sertório, a social democrat and an important opposition theorist, led the Seara Nova group in its break with the Directório. While adhering to a strategy of politicizing the masses through manifestoes, radio programs, and any peaceful means of disseminating information, the FPLN maintains ties with the African nationalist organizations.

Since 1962 the student movement has been the vanguard of dissent to the Salazar dictatorship. Demonstrations have won few concessions and reforms and resulted in death, bloodshed, and arrests and imprisonment of hundreds but have served to focus the nation's attention on problems at home and in the colonies. Since 1930 the Salazar regime had attempted to regulate all student life. The establishment of the youth movement, Mocidade Portuguesa (compulsory for all children from age seven to thirteen) assured the firm and disciplined control of the Portuguese youth. The first sign of organized protest among students appeared in 1945 with the establishment of the youth branch of the Movimento de Unidade Democrático, the MUD Juvenil which existed until about 1957. Student demonstrations in Lisbon occurred in early 1952, 1953, and 1957, the latter in protest against the regime's decree seeking to ban student associations. Delgado's electoral campaign in 1958, the hijacking of the luxury liner Santa Maria by Henrique Galvão, the outbreak of disorder in Angola, the loss of Goa in 1961, and the Beja uprising in early 1962 led to student demonstrations in March 1962 and thereafter. The initial demands for autonomy and reform evolved into a deep dissatisfaction with dictatorial order in Portugal and Africa. Politicized by their confrontation with that order, the impatient Portuguese youth, generally from well-to-do families, ideologically moved leftward to coalesce into dissident groups of Christian Socialist and Marxist orientation.

Both organized labor and the peasantry remain ineffective as political forces pressuring for change. The New State undermined the labor movement in the 1930's, reorganizing it into a controlled corporative framework of national syndicates. As in the past, the peasantry remains illiterate, apathetic, and apolitical, although increased emigration is a result of discontent in the countryside. The Catholic Action has had limited success in attempting to organize both the peasantry and urban labor.

The modern history of the trade union movement stems from the middle of the nineteenth century. Influenced by anarcho-syndicalism and socialism, the movement rapidly gained strength among industrial workers, and by the turn of the century strikes challenged the monarchy and contributed to the later republican chaos. In the 1930's legislation created the corporate system of employer and employee associations engaged in the same or affiliated class of economic, social, or professional activity. Employer associations, called *grêmios and sindicatos,* had been organized into corporations in their fields of activity. It was found impracticable to organize agricultural laborers and fishermen (the largest groups within the working class) into *sindicatos;* instead *Casas do Povo* and *Casas dos Pescadores* were established.

Since 1934, when workers in Lisbon launched a general strike, hundreds of labor disorders in the urban centers and rural areas have symbolized labor's disenchantment with the regime and focused attention on ever worsening conditions. In 1961 the Banco Nacional Ultramarino released statistics revealing the plight of the Portuguese worker. Based on average daily earnings of $1.26, it was estimated that the unskilled Lisbon laborer worked 20 minutes to earn a pound of bread and about 30 minutes for a pound of rice. In contrast, the farm worker with average daily earnings of $.85 worked 30 minutes to earn a pound of bread, three hours for a pound of second-grade beef, 25 hours for a pair of shoes, and 160 hours for a suit of appropriate quality. To support the military in Africa, in 1961 the government levied taxes on beer, soft drinks, tobacco, liquor, and other items, thereby further pressuring the low-income working and lower middle classes who long had been discontented with general economic conditions and the government's maintenance of stabilized wages.

Another problem, considered serious by the regime, is that of rapidly increasing emigration. Officially, about fifty thousand Portuguese leave annually; the actual emigration may be double that figure. Although agreements regarding Portuguese emigrants have been signed with the Netherlands, France, and Germany, bureaucratic red tape and a reluctance to allow a large outflow of Portuguese abroad have resulted in substantial illegal emigration.

Emigration among agricultural workers is highest. In the past, low levels of agricultural productivity have been accompanied by a surplus of cheap labor, which for the agricultural worker meant low wages, frequent unemployment, and increased exploitation. In recent years, there has been an exodus from countryside to urban areas and to foreign countries. Meanwhile, the agricultural sector remains stagnated by low productivity, ill-conceived attempts at mechanization, and improper planning. Today a lack of manpower on the farms is caused not only by the migration to cities and emigration abroad, but by recruiting for the expanding armed forces in the colonies. The regime also desires that emigrants move to the African colonies to bolster the ranks of the white minorities there.

In Africa, where conditions are worse than in the metropole, labor outside the subsistence economy is allocated into four categories: correctional labor, applicable in Moçambique for failure to pay the native head tax;

obligatory or conscripted labor utilized by the government for public works projects when insufficient volunteer workers are available; contract labor (often referred to as "forced labor"), required of Africans not employed for at least six months of the previous year; and voluntary labor for workers who contract directly with their employers. Portugal's labor problem in the colonies is a shortage of workers caused by the Moçambicans who migrate to the mining districts of the Transvaal and Angolans who are recruited for work on the cocoa plantations of São Tomé and Príncipe. Furthermore, although African labor is cheap, it is also largely unskilled and comparatively unproductive. From the African viewpoint, the labor market has been exploited and, as in Portugal, prevented from organizing in defense of basic human rights. Angolan, Guinean, and Moçambican nationalists recognize the necessity for backing the mass of native workers and have established representative organizations which, while exiled outside the Portuguese territories, remain ineffective and insignificant in the labor movement.

A Framework for Change

The alternatives for change in the African territories are, of course, related to the nationalist struggles as well as to political, economic, social, and cultural conditions in Portugal and to the institutional forces in favor of and opposed to the Salazar regime. Such alternatives are also related to external conditions and to the international scene. Three basic developments can be emphasized.

First, African nationalists achieved varying degrees of success in their struggle for independence. In Cabinda and in the northern Angolan regions of the Portuguese Congo, Dembos, and Malange, Africans were mobilized sporadically into an anti-colonial war. Although contained by the Portuguese deployment of massive troop forces and superior weaponry and military equipment, the African had not only awakened Portugal to its colonial responsibilities but politicized large segments of the indigenous population toward independence objectives. In Guiné nationalists claimed effective control over half the territory, while in Moçambique, Africans announced their domination over three of four provinces in which they were fighting. Weakened by a lack of financial resources and military training and equipment but bolstered by the commitment to end colonialism, the nationalists pinned their hopes on Guinean independence in the near future. They argued that an independent Guiné would provide them with a base from which to step up the war effort in Angola and Moçambique.

The inevitability of change in Portugal's political order was the greatest challenge confronting the New State's hold on the African territories. It appeared that any political alteration would be effected by supporters of the regime—the armed forces, the oligarchy, or the Church—and that liberal Catholic elements represented one important pressure favoring change and development.

Salazar's death or ouster would disrupt the old order. A conservative regime led by the army and supported by the oligarchy and Church hierarchy would be an immediate possibility, for Salazar had not chosen a successor. Other alternatives were few. A constitutional monarchy probably would not work because the administrative abilities of the pretender were doubtful and his popularity not great. A return to republicanism and rule by pragmatic politicians might lead to chaos. A shift to the extreme left was not likely. A coalition of elements supporting rapid social change and development was perhaps necessary if not a feasible alternative.

External pressure by the United Nations and, in particular, by the United States could serve to alter the current stalemate in Portugal and Portuguese Africa. Influenced principally by the Afro-Asian block of newly independent nations, the United Nations pressured for independence in the African territories. The effectiveness of the United Nations, however, was offset by the formidable southern bloc of African territories, including the Portuguese possessions and racist-ruled Rhodesia and South Africa. Another obstacle was the United States, whose policy was directed toward the preservation of cordial relations, the *status quo*, and economic interests in Portugal and southern Africa. A willingness on the part of the United States to pressure its NATO ally into granting eventual independence to the African colonies might affect diplomatic and military relations, especially the status of the U.S. bases on the Açores. Nevertheless, such pressure undoubtedly would cause internal repercussions, resulting perhaps in the collapse of the dictatorship and a modification of policy and relations with the African territories.

THREE

NATIONALISM AND DEVELOPMENT

Nationalism holds mystical and practical significance for developed and underdeveloped countries alike. As a concept for the scholarly study of the processes of change and development, however, nationalism must be carefully defined. Four tendencies may be identified as a basis for a working definition.

First, there is the traditional manifestation of nationhood prompted by a declaration of independence from colonial rule, the recognition of a geographical entity, and the obsession with protection of that entity's borders and resources. Portugal achieved such independence early in the twelfth century. Their contention that the overseas territories are "provinces," not colonies of the mother country, represents a second nationalistic trait—that of integral or supranationalism characterized by a mystical unity that links the colonies and the metropole into a single nation. Although not so definitive in the Portuguese case, integral nationalism frequently is associated with racial consciousness, exemplified by the aryan cult of the German fascist, the "pure" Indian culture of Andean Peru, and Black Muslimism. The Portuguese claim of racial harmony based on miscegenation and a civilizing policy was rudely discredited by the uprising in Angola during 1961. Such a claim is refuted by centuries of African resistance to the Portuguese. Indeed there seems to be historical justification that the black African resistance to white Portuguese rule itself is a manifestation of integral nationalism.

A third characteristic of nationalism is the desire to industrialize rapidly, especially in urban areas; industrialization, according to advocates of this nationalism, is brought about through a nation's exploitation of its natural resources and a break with traditional economic ties. A fourth component is radical nationalism represented by liberation movements desiring independence from colonialism or from oligarchic neocolonialism. Most exiled African movements presently fighting the Portuguese fall into this category.

Viewed collectively, these four traits represent only a partial definition of nationalism. By characterizing traditional nationalism as political, integral as cultural, industrial as economic and radical as social, however, the concept becomes useful as a theoretical framework within which may be examined nations' problems revolving around such phenomena as structural change and development. Structural change and development involve shifts and modifications among national political, economic, social, and cultural institutions—thus the relationship of nationalism to change and development. Stated more precisely, nationalism can be viewed as developmental nationalism. In an ideological context, developmental nationalism offers modernizing nations a critique of the old political, economic, social, and cultural order. To be effective, developmental nationalism also draws the general outlines of the ideal substitute for that order. Emancipation from political subordination, economic exploitation, and the barriers of social stratification allows for a recasting of a new order, not necessarily by violent means, but by shifts among institutional forces that allow for mobility and a recognition of societal demands. Structural change and development may be accompanied by an awareness or consciousness that emanates from broad sectors of society that are alienated from and opposed to the traditional order. These "awakened" sectors are imbued with the desire to reshape society as a whole. Through communications, leaders mobilize these broad emergent sectors to work together for national objectives and goals and to escape from traditional backwardness.

Societies generally move from traditional to transitional and eventually to modern stages of development. Traditional, regional, linguistic, and cultural values are affected by rapid and intensive communications at the national level, thereby allowing for assimilation of transitional and modern values. Traditional authorities are eclipsed, and national symbols are forged. Migratory shifts of peoples from rural to urban areas are accompanied by social mobilization that welds individuals and groups together and instills in them an allegiance to symbols of national identity and an awareness of nationhood. In this process exchange economies replace subsistence agriculture; national markets absorb local market systems. Mobilization of manpower contributes to the effective accumulation of economic resources. The modernizing society develops a capacity to redirect or form new combinations of economic, social, and human resources. Thus, as societies approach modernization, they acquire political viability, a sense of social justice, and an orientation toward political, economic, social, and cultural change and development. A new pattern of cohesiveness and integration emerges. Utilizing developmental nationalism as a model, let us examine more closely the phenomenon labeled nationalism first by the Portuguese, then by the African in Portuguese Africa.

Portuguese Nationalism

The Portuguese are bound by a sense of unity and the idea of community that identifies the individual with the nation. Although there are common historical traditions, language, religion, literature, symbols, and experiences, Portuguese nationalism does not fit our model of developmental nationalism as has been illustrated in the preceding chapter.

Portuguese nationalism is characterized by a mysticism kindled by the emulation of renowned past exploits of valor. Many Portuguese writers trace the Portuguese spirit of nationality to the revolt of Viriatus, the Lusitanian shepherd who resisted the Romans in the second century B.C. It may be asserted, however, that Christianity and the medieval Crusades against the Moors contributed to the early basis of national union. A geographer, Dan Stanislawski, adopts the thesis that Portuguese individuality can be attributed to the persistent historical and cultural differences between the northwest and the neighboring Spanish tableland, the *meseta*. Besides the cultural and physical differences that existed between the humid periphery of the peninsula and the *meseta*, Stanislawski (in *The Individuality of Portugal*) argues that the border between Portugal and Spain runs through zones of disinterest; that northwest Portugal, where nationhood was established, was politically isolated during the several centuries prior to independence; and that internal dissension and wars among the meseta kingdoms diverted attention from Portugal.

Portugal's adherence to past exploits was described by V. Bragança-Cunha as both "the cradle and the grave of Portuguese greatness," and by the literary critic and writer, Fidelino de Figueiredo, as the excessive glorification of an epic spirit which, "though appealing, is highly misleading."

Aubrey Bell, the British critic and admirer of Portuguese literature and life, characterized the Portuguese as diligent workers who bravely endure hardships, combine loyalty with determination, and "accept a situation which they may not like but with a pertinacious looking for better things, persistent rather than restless." They are instilled with "a contented melancholy, a resigned, genial pessimism, and a patient, perhaps indolent tolerance, finding relief in sarcasm and irony." Bell adds that the most fundamentally Portuguese characteristic is a certain wistful melancholy or *saudade* . . . a vague and constant desire for something that does not and probably cannot exist for something other than the present, a turning towards the past or towards the future; not an active discontent or poignant sadness but an indolent dreaming wistfulness.

This behavior is linked directly to the mystique of imperial destiny that has caught the imagination of Portuguese policymakers during past centuries. Initially national consolidation and identity at home were extended to embrace the overseas discoveries and expansion—prompted by Portugal's ready access to the sea, the inertia of the struggle against the Moors, and the foresight of Prince Henry the Navigator. Portugal's mariners not only discovered the world but fulfilled a special "mission" to transmit Catholicism and Lusitanian civilization to remote peoples. According to the official view, Christian ideals are linked inseparably to Portuguese values and patriotism. The imparting of Portuguese values to tropical Africa is fundamental to the civilizing mission. The chief value is nationhood, conceived of as a pan-Lusitanian community stretching around the world and embracing many races into a mystical cultural unity. The destiny of Africans in the overseas territories is resolved by adherence to Portuguese nationalism, thereby denying all efforts to achieve independence.

The Portuguese position on nationalism at home and overseas can be summed up as follows: Portugal, the oldest of nations in Europe maintaining original territorial boundaries, since independence in the twelfth century has been blessed with a sense of mission. To remain independent, Portugal under the guidance of Henry the Navigator had to expand across the seas. Indeed Portuguese exploration and conquest saved Africa for Europe and liberated the continent from Arab domination. Their multiracial origin gave the Portuguese a special capacity to live in all kinds of climates and conditions and to assimilate all peoples of all races into one nation or provinces scattered about the world. The basis of Portuguese life stems from an old communal society based on a complex group of families organized into a patriarchal structure. The rule of community was entrusted to a council comprised of heads of families who elected among themselves special authorities to whom power was entrusted. Although the old communal society has given way to progress, the family aggregate remains intact, and the Portuguese live in harmony with their traditions and with a sense of common origin.

The heterogeneous composition of the Portuguese and the traditional community and patriarchal structure allowed the complete assimilation of the Christian spirit of fraternity. Thus harmony has always characterized the policy of the nation and the behavior of its individuals. The Portuguese did not conquer but established friendly relations with various peoples. Through enforcement of the principle of hierarchical authority, administrators and missionaries achieved cohesion among the parts of the widely dispersed nation. In Portuguese Africa, white and black mingle with national fervor and pride, a sense of cultural unity, identity of interests and aspirations that coalesce disparate elements in the Lusitanian community. In Africa and throughout the empire the presence of the Portuguese nation is effective and proclaimed by the patriotism of the people. Everywhere the Portuguese have brought indigenous peoples into contact with civilization.

The Portuguese must preserve this historical heritage and maintain continuity and solidarity with past, present, and future. Survival of order in Africa is dependent on the moral unity of the Portuguese. There is no difference in views between Portuguese of the metropole and those overseas. For this reason problems which are insurmountable for others do not arise for the Portuguese, who rely upon each other and whose moral unity is strengthened by trust in hierarchal authority and confidence in the unbreakable alliance of all Portuguese in the Lusitanian community.

The Portuguese position is spelled out in the legislation of the New State. The constitution, Salazar's personal creation, states that "the Nation fulfill its historic mission of colonization in the lands of the Discoveries . . . and to diffuse among the population inhabiting them the benefits of their civilization." In the 1961 decree abolishing the controversial "Estatuto dos Indígenas" traditional policy is emphasized: "The heterogeneous composition of the Portuguese people, its traditional structure of a communal and patriarchal character, and the Christian ideal of brotherhood always present in our overseas expansion, soon marked our policy toward other societies and cultures and imbued it from the start with a deep respect for the usage and customs of the populations we encountered." Apologists argue that this legislation and other decrees promulgated by the New State, symbolize Salazar's greatest achievement—the raising of Portugal's prestige internationally, by instilling the Portuguese with a consciousness of their national and imperial destiny and with an attachment to the notion of Lusitanian community.

Lusotropicology: A Defense of the Portuguese Position

Utilizing the Portuguese assumptions of national integration, Gilberto Freyre, the Brazilian sociologist, postulates the concept of Lusotropicology as a basis for systematic study of ecological and social integration in tropical environment. His thesis, developed in a series of studies published by the Portuguese government and others, is a substantial defense of official policy in Africa. This thesis, concisely summarized, states that with the Portuguese expansion in the fifteenth century a new type of civilization began. Since that time the Portuguese have been transforming the tropics, not by introducing European values but by themselves changing into Lusotropicals in body and soul. Integration tended to harmonize and to unify detached or disintegrated elements of society. Integration was achieved in part through miscegenation and in part through socially Christianizing non-Europeans rather than culturally Europeanizing them.

The Portuguese experience in the African world contributed to the emergence of a Lusotropical civilization characterized by the biological process of interpenetration of cultures. The conspicuous model of an evolving Lusotropical civilization is found in the Cape Verde islands, where a mixed race developed because of the isolation of the archipelago and a prolific miscegenation between white Portuguese and black Africans. Portuguese studies confirm the belief that the Cape Verdean is "the most perfect Portuguese human being," that the fusion of European and African produced a racial and social harmony unknown elsewhere in the tropics. Brazil also represents a model for Lusotropicalism, according to Freyre. There a regime of slave labor with a patriarchal character and softened by a Christian inspiration lasted until the late nineteenth century and served to consolidate a Lusotropical civilization, characterized by the protection granted the slave by his master and by the opportunity for the slave to participate in community life. Brazil evolved as an advanced ethnic democracy. Although it remains predominantly European in style, its culture has absorbed many African and some Asian values from segments of its population. Freyre asserts therefore that Brazil is in an ideal position to influence development of the new Afro-Asian nations and to assume leadership of tropical nations with problems common to Brazilian experience.

Although Brazilian nationalists accept the assertion that their nation is destined to assume the leadership of the tropical world, most disagree with Freyre's assumption that Portuguese colonial policy and influence nourished development of Brazil. Furthermore, most Brazilian nationalists insist that the present Portuguese policy of exploitation cannot result in the establishment of new "Brazils" in Africa. The Brazilian historian, José Honório Rodrigues, is the leading proponent of this view. Rodrigues credits the African Negro with playing an important economic and cultural role, while miscegenation was a decisive factor in the ethnic formation of Brazil, which is neither aboriginized nor Africanized, but balanced and homogeneous. This view comes close to the Freyre thesis. However, whereas Freyre attempts to demonstrate that miscegenation and societal cohesion are evidences of Portuguese characteristics, Rodrigues shows that such characteristics are essentially Brazilian.

Presumably the position of Rodrigues and other nationalists prompted the Brazilian government's negative reaction in late 1965 to a Portuguese proposal for establishment of a commonwealth of all Portuguese-speaking peoples. In effect, Portugal was calling for formal recognition of the Lusitanian community. Although in the 1950's Brazilian President Juscelino Kubitschek had maintained close diplomatic ties with Portugal, such a foreign policy was obscured by Jânio Quadros and João Goulart, who supported African demands for self-determination and opposed Portugal's rule in Africa. Close ties between Portugal and Brazil were reestablished in 1964 under the military rule of Humberto Castelo Branco. Castelo Branco denounced the policy of his predecessors and affirmed that the spirit of historical traditions in the civilizing mission of Portugal would allow for solutions to problems in Africa. Castelo Branco supported the idea of a Portuguese-speaking commonwealth but preferred that Brazil assume a prestigious role as mediator between Portugal and Africa, a position unacceptable to Portugal.

African Nationalism

Since the fifteenth century African resistance has challenged Portugal's imperial design. Today Africans advocating independence and nationhood are deeply conscious of their exploited past. A history of African resistance to the Portuguese has yet to be written. What literature is available concerns Portuguese policy, role, and achievements—for the most part written from the Portuguese point of view.

African nationalism began to evolve in the Portuguese territories in the late 1940's and early 1950's; not until the early 1960's, however, did nationalism serve as the impetus for direct action and struggle for independence. After World War II, a small elite of African intellectuals found their way to universities in Lisbon and Coimbra. These were the assimilated or "civilized" Africans educated in the Portuguese language, history, and geography. This educated elite represented the New State's efforts to build a colonial culture. In the overseas territories this elite had been allowed participation in legal associations established by the government for the "assimilados."

The first such association, the Liga Africana, was formed in Lisbon in 1923 as a government-sponsored organization. Six years later in Luanda the Liga Nacional Africana and the Grêmio Africano, later called the Associação Regional dos Naturais de Angola, were founded. A similar pattern emerged in Moçambique, where the Associação Africana and the Centro Associativo dos Negros de Moçambique were established respectively for assimilated mulatto and black Africans. The Associação dos Naturais de Moçambique was created for and continues to be dominated by Europeans born in Moçambique. Africans manifested demands through these organizations by urging moderate reforms in the 1930's and focusing discussion on direct participation for the urban masses in the 1940's. The government reacted by replacing elected leaders with administrative appointees and by dominating and interfering with the activities of these organizations.

By the middle 1950's clandestine political movements were formed in Angola, Guiné, and Moçambique. At the same time, African intellectuals studying at Portuguese universities established the Movimento Anti-Colonista (MAC) as an outgrowth of the controversial Casa dos Estudantes do Império, the semi-official center for Africans in Lisbon that was condemned as subversive and closed by the government in 1965. A few of these intellectuals such as the Angolan, Mário de Andrade, and the Moçambican, Marcelino dos Santos, left Portugal and settled in Paris where they associated with French African advocates of *négritude* and others who sought an African culture, traditional in tone but modern and sophisticated in content. Their affinity to European cultural and materialistic values denied them an identity which truly could be characterized as pure Africanism.

As such, *négritude* was theoretical and also superficial. It inspired poets, historians, and others to convene the first congress of black African writers and artists in Paris in 1956 and to establish the Société Africaine de Culture and its American affiliate, the American Society of African Culture as well as the important cultural journal, *Présence Africaine*. Andrade and Santos were associated with these organizations.

In 1960 at the second All-African Peoples Congress, held in Tunis, the MAC was superseded by the Frente Revolucionária Africana para a Independência das Colônias Portuguesas (FRAIN). In April 1961 the FRAIN was dissolved and replaced by the Confederação das Organizações Nacionalistas das Colónias Portuguesas (CONCP). The CONCP, a coordinating organization working for unity of nationalist movements struggling against the Portuguese, advocates an end to Portuguese colonialism and immediate independence of the African territories.

Several patterns thus emerged in the historical evolution of African nationalism. First, the government's favoring of a "civilized" elite of African intellectuals served to divide "civilized" Africans from the "natives." This privileged elite at first found itself compromised to Portuguese colonial policy and unable to defend the interests of the African community. The African elite, comprised mostly of mulattoes, became elevated into a value and ideal. As in Brazil, according to the thesis of Freyre, racial mixture reduced racial strife and led to cultural affinity between white and black. This writer's interviews with African nationalists in 1965 revealed a conciliatory attitude among those who had been exposed to Portuguese life and culture. Despite an intransigent Portuguese policy that resulted in their harassment, imprisonment, and eventual exile, many nationalists affirmed a respect for the Portuguese people and for the Portuguese language, customs, and cultural heritage.

Second, despite this apparent assimilation of African and European cultural values, the mulatto intelligentsia attempted to move beyond the Freyre thesis of Lustotropicology as well as the new style of behavior, *négritude*, for negrification of the African not only involved the respect for sophisticated European culture but required the glorification of the Negro in Africa and an awareness of his aesthetic values. Accordingly, *négritude* became Africanitude, thereby challenging Lusotropical theory as the mulatto intelligentsia became disenchanted with Portuguese mystique and began identifying itself with the urban and rural masses in Portuguese Africa. There is little literature available to support this assumption, although Mário de Andrade, an Angolan intellectual, rebutted the Freyre thesis many years ago. Andrade denounced Lusotropicalism as a myth. In reality, he argued, the Portuguese policy of assimilation assured both "segregation and a systematic limitation of social ascension" in the African territories. He supported his view by reference to the 1950 census which revealed that less than one per cent of black Africans had achieved "civilized" status.

A third historical pattern of nationalism reveals that the African elite radicalized its position in reaction to Portuguese administrative policy that fostered forced labor, illiteracy, economic and social misery, and racial discrimination against the masses. Slowly, nationalism evolved in a stifled atmosphere of secrecy. Failure to mobilize the African urban masses through strikes and sabotage in the late 1950's, however, resulted in a shift in tactics and strategy involving revolutionary action. Nationalist leaders appealed to the rural peasantry to organize into guerrilla units and armies to overthrow colonialism and Portuguese oppression. Such was the experience of Amílcar Cabral's movement in Guiné. Utilizing Cabral's experience, Eduardo Mondlane and Moçambican nationalists mobilized the natives of northern Moçambique into a clandestine network of effective resistance to Portuguese rule. Agostinho Neto and Angolan intellectuals failed in the early 1960's to achieve effective mobilization of the rural masses. In contrast, Holden Roberto, who unlike Cabral, Mondlane, and Neto was not educated in Portuguese universities, led tens of thousands of black Angolans in revolt. Roberto, a black African, however, had lived most of his life in Léopoldville, and his movement was comprised of Africans from northern Angola—facts supporting the contention that the movement was regionally, not nationally oriented.

A fourth pattern evolved as the African accepted militant and revolutionary alternatives in the independence struggle. As the abyss widened between African and Portuguese, nationalists began to work out developmental schemes that could be utilized once independence was assured. Their revolution and aspirations for nationhood made them aware of the complex structural problems ahead. Their desire for change and development was accompanied by concrete and rational solutions for political, economic, social, and cultural problems. In theory, many of these African leaders envisaged a model approaching that of developmental nationalism. In the political sector they seemed to accept a charismatic leader and a single "mass" political party as the basis for aggregating and recruiting formerly nonparticipating groups and individuals into national life. Economic resources, mainly agriculture, would be fully exploited and foreign capital probably nationalized where monopolies prevailed. Income redistribution and full employment would occur as the government centralized control over the economy. Education would be available to all. Literacy campaigns would mobilize the people into a cohesive national force.

It is too early to speculate whether the African can and will fulfill his objectives of development and nationalism. It is safe to assume, however, that circumstantial events, influenced greatly by Portuguese intransigent policies, awakened the privileged African intelligentsia to challenge the Portuguese hegemony in Africa. Africans are conscious of the problems of traditional order. They seek new alternatives for Portuguese Africa. They desire to reshape their societies and to mobilize mass sectors to work together for national objectives and goals. They are oriented toward structural change, development, and modernization and are striving for national cohesiveness and integration.

FOUR

ANGOLA

Although the Portuguese first reached the Angolan coast at the end of the fifteenth century, several centuries passed before they penetrated and effectively occupied that territory of West Central Africa. Concentrating along the coast, they encountered difficulty in overcoming the inland climatic conditions, tropical disease, and resistance of the native African. To a large extent the history of Angola has been patterned after Portuguese commercial relations with the African, for the Portuguese explorers and traders sought minerals, ivory, and slaves and in the process disrupted indigenous economies. The role of the missionary also affected historical developments.

Geography too played a role as Portuguese attention was first directed to the Congo kingdom of the north, which was treated as a friendly ally. Because of inattention and lack of resources, the Portuguese lost control over the Congo, adopted a militant policy, and turned south to the conquest of the Angolan kingdoms which were subdued after one hundred years of war. Luanda became the center of Portuguese control and penetration of the interior. From Luanda, economic expansion and colonialism was carried further south to Benguela and beyond. Military expeditions reached inland from Benguela as far as the Ovimbundu kingdoms which succumbed to Portuguese domination. In the Humbe and Huíla regions in southern Angola it took Portugal several decades of humiliating defeats before establishing its authority.

By the early twentieth century the military campaigns of pacification established Portuguese hegemony over its colony of Angola. This hegemony gave Africans a semblance of unity (the Portuguese language, for example, provided a common basis for communication), but it also accompanied a dispersed indigenous society and insignificant development as Portugal struggled with internal political disorder and economic difficulties at home. These conditions culminated in African outbreaks, first in Luanda during February 1961 and throughout northern Angola a month later,

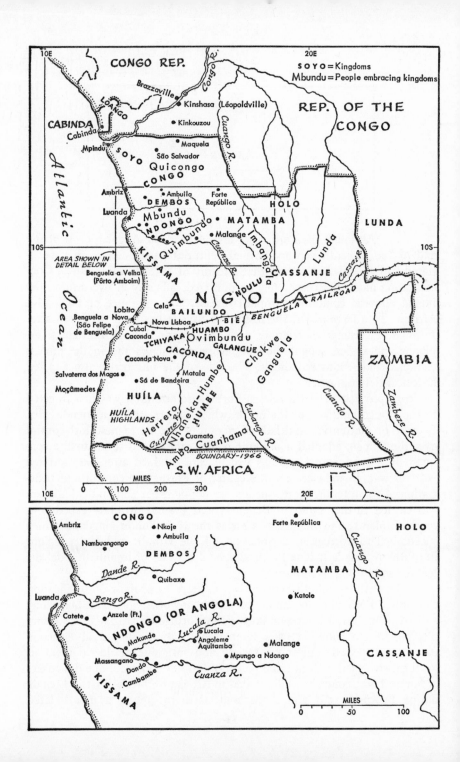

which awakened the Portuguese to the complacency and mystique which had long characterized their presence in the territory.

Fragmentation and Disruption

Disruptive elements contribute to societal fragmentation in Angola. Important among these elements are geographical dissimilarities, discrimination provoking reaction among both Europeans and native Africans in Angola, ethnic differences in the traditional tribal order, conflict between Roman Catholic and Protestant missions over their education roles, a large African refugee population residing outside Angola, an official policy of colonization that encourages and favors white settlement while generally ignoring the black African population, and an exploitative pattern of European development oriented more to raw material extraction than to territorial industrialization. An examination of these elements tends to support the initial assumption that fragmentation and disruption are evident in Angola today.

A first consideration is geographical, for Angola is a large territory (fourteen times the area of Portugal) bordered by the Republic of the Congo to the north and northeast, by Zambia to the east and by South-West Africa to the south. A narrow coastal strip, stretching about one thousand miles in length and little more than one hundred miles at its widest, contrasts with a series of plateaus and tablelands to the interior which reach elevations of four to seven thousand feet before falling away to the east. Although the whole of the territory lies within the tropics, large segments of the southern coast, influenced by the cold Benguela current, are dry and desert-like while the high altitudes of the interior provide for cool climatic conditions and also give the territory a perennial river system. From the Benguela highland flow innumerable rivers, including the head waters of such systems as the Zambeze, Cassai, Cunene, and Cuanza. Further north is the highland region of Malange, inland from the coastal plain of lowlands stretching to the southern bank of the Congo mouth. To the south and inland from Moçâmedes are the Huíla highlands and their capital Sá de Bandeira. Luanda and Lobito are excellent harbors, the latter (with the Benguela Railway) linking the coast with the highland interior and the mineral riches of Katanga in the Congo (also with Zambia, although presently copper exports from that country filter through the Moçambique port of Beira). Thus geographically, Angola is both diverse and expansive.

These geographical aspects partially account for a divisiveness in Angola's populations. The territory is sparsely populated, owing principally to the repercussions of the slave trade of past centuries and to discriminatory labor practices (something similar to slavery) in recent times. The impact of that slave trade and labor practices resulted in shifts in power structure among African tribal chiefs who cooperated with the Portuguese in promoting slave outlets along the coast. Not infrequently did the Portuguese send their *pombeiros* (European but almost invariably mulatto or black African traders or emissaries) into the interior to stir up a local war in expectation of being able to buy the prisoners. Thus began a pattern of pitting tribe against tribe and sometimes favoring one tribe over another. Such a pattern, which continues today, served the Portuguese purpose of dividing the African ranks to erode mass identification with a common protest against the Portuguese.

A startling feature of the roughly five million inhabitants of Angola was the rapid growth of the European population during recent decades (about four hundred per cent between 1940 and 1960) which, although representing less than five per cent of the total, tended to support Portugal's tenuous hold on the territory. This expanding white minority, however, merged into an "indigenous" European society whose own nationalist perspective favored Angola's separation from the metropole, not simply because of geographical distance but because of the territory's great potential for economic development and a preference to trade with foreign countries owing to the limitations of Portuguese markets. As early as 1860 and in the 1890's and 1920's separatist tendencies were manifested by white settlers who demanded administrative and financial autonomy as well as economic development. In the 1960's a Frente Unida Angolense (FUA) issued similar demands. Their cause for concern was partially attributed to prevalent discriminatory attitudes by the Portuguese administrative officials against Angolan Europeans over a period of many years.

Traditional tribal structure and ethnic differentiation disrupt the social order. The majority of the native population is of Bantu origin; small numbers of Hottentots and Bushmen reside in southern Angola. The largest ethnic group (estimated 1.5 million population) is the Umbundu-speaking Ovimbundu (generally referred to as the Bailundos by the Portuguese) whose home is the central highlands of Angola. Gladwyn Childs names thirteen Umbundu-speaking kingdoms as well as nine tributary kingdoms. Linguistically the Ovimbundu belong with their southern neighbors, including the Ambo and Herrero, while their northern and eastern neighbors relate to other language groups (Umbundu should not be confused with the Quimbundo-speaking groups of the Ndongo or Angola kingdoms). Through the legends of the Ovimbundu, Childs identifies the remote and peaceful highland country of Ndulu as one of the oldest Umbundu kingdoms, probably established as a refuge from the prolonged wars between the Portuguese and the kingdom of Ndongo.

Adrian Edwards writes that the Ovimbundu are a fusion of "Jagas" (a conquering race that invaded the Benguela highlands in the sixteenth and seventeenth centuries) and the indigenous peoples of southwest Angola. Today the Ovimbundu live under the economic, political, and religious system introduced and maintained by Europeans. In the late nineteenth century their trade with Europeans was in rubber and slaves, the latter becoming intensified in the period after 1890. Their crafts being inferior, the Ovimbundu became dependent on the Portuguese for clothes, guns, rum, and other goods. In exchange for these goods they traded their main crop, maize. Until the end of their independence in the early twentieth century the Ovimbundu were divided into several kingdoms with Bailundo, the largest, being subdivided into some two hundred chiefdoms. The Ovimbundu were positively responsive to Catholic and Protestant missionaries alike, and acceptance of Christianity by many resulted in a closer tie to Europeans and a feeling of superiority to other African peoples, all of which contributed to Ovimbundu subservience to and, at times, cooperation with the Portuguese.

A second group, the Quimbundo (or Kimbundu), comprises roughly 1.1 million inhabitants who occupy a rectangular area from Luanda eastwards. They are strongly influenced by European values, are dependent on the urban economy of Luanda and Malange, and generally speak Portuguese. From this group has emerged an African intelligentsia whose nationalist-oriented leadership resides in exile and desires independence. The most notable of Quimbundo kingdoms was that of the Mbundu people, whose kingdom of Ndongo or Angola (their king was known as Ngola) the Portuguese conquered during the seventeenth century.

The Quicongo (or Kikongo) group numbers one half million who occupy the Portuguese Congo of northern Angola. Ethnically they overlap territorial borders and populate large districts in the two Congo republics. They are the descendants of the largest kingdom of pre-colonial West Central Africa, the Congo kingdom. Although divided by the Belgian, French, and Portuguese boundaries established in the colonial era, the Quicongo maintain some cultural unity (roughly half the population of northern Angola are refugees in the Congo). In Angola the Quicongo group comprises some fifteen peoples, including (in order of population size) the Baxicongos, Bassossos, Bazombos, Bassorongos, and Bacongos. The Bacongos, in particular, are linked with the Abako political party of the Congo, a party whose objectives have included restoration of the

Congo kingdom whose ancient site was the district of São Salvador. It was this area which became a center for the uprising staged in 1961 and maintained thereafter.

Another ethnic group is the Lunda-Chokwe (360,000 population). Occupying a northeastern section of Angola, the Lunda are relatively isolated, although many find employment in the diamond mines of the region. The Chokwe, known as hunters and traders, are scattered, having spread westward across southern Umbundu and northern Nhaneka-Humbe (see below) territory and westward across Katanga in the Congo and Zambia.

Other ethnic groups include the Ganguela or Nganguela (330,000 population) whose heterogeneous subgroups use such names as Luimbes, Luenas, Luvales, and Bundas; the Nhaneka-Humbe group (200,000 population), culturally related to their northern neighbors, the Ovimbundu, but resistant to European assimilation; the Ambo group (63,000 population) within which the principal people is the Cuanhama (Kuanyama or Kwanyama) who were victims of the Portuguese conquest of their region of southern Angola and the massacre of 1904 (the capital of the Ambo is in this region although most Ambo peoples live in South-West Africa); the Herrero (25,000 population), a cattle-raising people in desert regions of southern Angola, South-West Africa, and Botswana; and the previously mentioned non-Bantu group of other peoples, including the Hottentot-Bushman.

The social order has been both strongly influenced and disrupted by missionary activities in Angola. Before the promulgation of new reforms in September 1961, the Portuguese government considered itself responsible for educating only the European and "civilized" population of the overseas territories. The Roman Catholic Church, partially supported by government funds, was charged with the responsibility of educating the "native" African population. In December 1921 the government decreed that only Portuguese would be used for primary education and that annual subsidies would be granted to qualified European teachers in the mission and rural schools. Prior to that time the government had not concerned itself with educating the African population. Four decades later a system of "rudimentary education" was inaugurated, a system which was entrusted to the Catholic missions. Owing to the lack of economic resources and personnel, however, the Catholic Church failed substantially to alter the prevalent pattern of illiteracy in the African population.

The Protestant Church long has been active in Angola, converting the natives to Christianity and providing education and health services, although it has received no government subsidies. The Baptist Missionary Society of London (active during the period 1878 to 1963) and four other Protestant missionary societies were strongly influential in the Quicongo region of northern Angola, where census figures acknowledged that 35 per cent of the population was Protestant. The societies were not officially recognized under Portuguese law and therefore were suspect and subject to governmental criticism after the March 1961 African rebellion. Perhaps justly accused of having stirred up nationalist sentiment in the region, the five societies were forced to withdraw all missionary personnel and close eight of ten stations. The reasons for the Portuguese censure of Protestantism can be related to the styles of life that differentiate Protestantism from Catholicism. Only a small minority of Portuguese are practicing Protestants. Furthermore, many of the leaders and participants in the 1961 rebellion had been schooled in the Protestant missions.

Thomas Okuma, a Protestant missionary, has suggested that the church has disrupted Angolan society because it "supplants traditional kings and elders as the highest authority." "Loyalty to the church," he argued, "comes to transcend kinship and tribal ties." He then noted parallels between African mass party structure and existing church (Protestant and Catholic) structure in Angola and hypothesized that mass parties could evolve from church organizations. Under such conditions, Okuma stated, religious organization could bring radical political consequences, including independence, to Angola.

The rebellion in northern Angola not only resulted in the exodus of most missionaries in the region but also in the flight of several hundred thousand Angolans to the former Belgian Congo. By May 1961 approximately 60,000 refugees had crossed the Angolan border; by December the number approached 150,000, according to United Nations statistics. By 1964 the total surpassed 350,000, and the numbers of refugees fleeing to the Congo continued to increase during 1965 and 1966. The United Nations and several private organizations provided assistance, especially during the early years of the rebellion.

The Angolan refugees fled in panic for many reasons. Principally they were terrified by the chaotic turn of events. Admittedly, a small percentage of refugees had been intimidated by the rebellious nationalists. The majority, however, apparently left Angola for fear of reprisal by Portuguese authorities, even though the latter had initiated a "pacification" campaign in late 1961 to win back their support. According to documented refugee accounts, the African initially was the victim of a campaign of mass extermination (tens of thousands were killed) by the Portuguese in Angola. There were many cases of atrocities, widespread arrests, and shootings by the police and military, along with air raids that included bombs and strafing. That few refugees returned to their homes in Angola attested to the seriousness of the situation.

Economically, Angola is primarily agricultural, evidence of which is reflected in its exports. Coffee accounts for nearly half the agricultural exports; others are corn, fish meal, cotton, sugar, and rice. Mineral exports, especially copper, petroleum, iron ore, and diamonds are of increasing importance. Although the Portuguese developmental plans are oriented toward infrastructure and eventual industrialization, both private and public capital have been directed to raw materials which are destined either to Portugal or to other European countries. As a result, internal industrialization has lagged, and despite abundant hydroelectric power, modern transport facilities are inadequate, skilled industrial workers scarce, and internal markets small as a result of low wages and insignificant demand for consumer goods. In fact, developmental plans are oriented to favor both the entrenched white oligarchy and the Portuguese population in the territory as well as the cliques of industrialists and financiers in the metropole and abroad who wield monopoly control over a large share of economic activity. For example, the Angola Mining Company, which holds a monopoly concession over a large region of Angola, is controlled by Belgian, South African, and Portuguese interests; a number of Portuguese companies (in cooperation with Belgian and U.S. interests) control exclusive rights to prospect for petroleum in large areas of Angola; and four companies (assisted by German and Danish capital) dominate rapidly expanding iron ore extraction. This recent economic activity, especially since 1961, was the subject of an investigating committee of the United Nations which in 1965 entitled its report, "The Activities of Foreign Economic and other Interests which Are Impeding . . . Independence in the Territories under Portuguese Administration." This report affirmed that mineral concessions and a large influx of domestic and foreign capital have allowed Portugal to hedge on the question of independence.

Despite expansion in some sectors, the Angolan economy was subject to fluctuations in world market prices of agricultural products (especially coffee) and also to dwindling foreign exchange reserves as a result of exemption of many enterprises from exchange restrictions. Although restrictions on the colonial economy were relaxed somewhat by reforms in 1961 and 1962, the agricultural sector continued to suffer from a lack of skilled labor. Furthermore, with little or no technical assistance and credit available, the African continued as a subsistence farmer, outside the market economy and relatively unaffected by Portugal's apparent attempt to develop the territory's economy. In effect, developmental plans were having little impact on the black African, who remained structured in his traditional situation and whose economic contribution was limited by wasteful cultivation practices, poor quality production, and a tendency to pursue migratory slash-and-burn techniques of farming. As such, the poor subsistence farming African was sharply differentiated from the Portuguese colonists on the plateaus (for whom credits and technical assistance were available) who cultivated such cash crops as wheat, cereal, and fruit and from the owners of large and medium size plantations who cultivated such export commodities as coffee, sugar, and sisal in the plateau regions, tobacco and cotton in the central plains, and fibers and palm oil in the enclave of Cabinda.

With trade unionism relatively unknown in Angola and the right to strike or protest forbidden, the African labor force lacked technical skills, and those employed in urban economies worked as unskilled common laborers or house servants. Generally the African labor force remained tied to the subsistence tribal economy. Many Africans were subject to the hardships of contract or recruited labor, which in turn disrupted African village life. In contrast, most of the skilled laborers were Europeans who were either born in Angola or emigrated from the overpopulated metropole.

The government's policy of encouraging Portuguese emigrants to settle in colonization projects also tended to disrupt the social order. Hundreds of families from Portugal were settled at Cela in the highlands northwest of Nova Lisboa, at Vila Folgares near Matala, east of Sá de Bandeira, and in the Bengo river valley, located north of Luanda. The government's colonization policy was designed to justify Portugal's continued presence in Angola in the face of an African majority that potentially threatened their presence. The colonization schemes were not altogether successful, however. Many of the Portuguese peasants were relatively unskilled. Their contribution to the economy and that of skilled European farmers was meager, and many tended to migrate to the cities. Essentially the government policy was racially motivated, undercutting the belief in a homogeneous multiracial society.

The Rise and Fall of the Congo Monarchy

Recorded historical developments of the Congo kingdoms can be sketched through several periods from the fifteenth century until the

1950's. According to Paiva Manso and Ernst Georg Ravenstein, the founder of the Congo dynasty was Ntinu Mini a Lukeni, who conquered numerous independent kinglets, established a capital at Mbanza Kongo (present-day São Salvador) and, as the paramount chief (Ntotela or Manicongo) of a loose confederation of six provinces, extended his conquests southward to the Cuanza and even beyond (to the kingdoms of Ndongo and Matamba). Sent north across the Congo river, his sons founded the kingdoms of the Kakongo and Loango. The fourth Ntotela to head the kingdom, Nkuwu a Nitinu, was also a son of Ntinu Nimi a Lukeni and in turn was succeeded by his own son, Nzinga a Nkuwu, or better known in history as João I, who with a son and other members of the court was baptized by the Portuguese in May 1491.

Nearly a decade earlier Diogo Cão had seized four Congo Africans whom he carried back to Portugal (his own four-man embassy had been retained by the Congo monarch) where they were received by João II as guests of the crown. To penetrate the interior of southern Africa (and hopeful of establishing contact with the kingdom of Prester John), the Portuguese decided to seek an alliance with the Congo kingdom. Exposed to Portuguese values and culture, the four Africans became messengers of goodwill who impressed their compatriots with tales of distant Portugal after triumphantly returning to the Congo about 1484. Nzinga a Nkuwu was receptive to the Portuguese visit and dispatched a small mission to Portugal to be trained in European ways. At the same time he requested João II to send missionaries and technicians to instruct his people.

In response to the African's request, João II ordered a peaceful expedition of three ships with priests and skilled workers whose purpose was not to conquer but to evangelize and seek alliance with Nzinga a Nkuwu. Although the Portuguese joined Nzinga in putting down a rebellion of the Anzico tribe, the cooperative venture languished after Vasco da Gama opened up a route to the promises of the East. The few Portuguese residents remaining in the Congo began to trade slaves with owners of São Tomé sugar plantations. At the same time internal strife plagued the Congo region. The converted African chief João I, influenced by his second son (perhaps nephew), Mpanzu a Nzinga (or Mpanzu a Kítima), reverted to his heathen ways and turned against his first son and heir apparent, Mbemba a Nzinga or Affonso I, and two priests who had concentrated their attention upon assuring his allegiance to the Portuguese cause. João I died about 1506, and Affonso succeeded to the throne after overcoming the opposition of his brother, who was captured and decapitated.

The long reign of Affonso I (1507-1543?) was marked by his desire to bring European civilization to his kingdom. Such intent was marred by his paradoxical acceptance of an export slave trade which caused internal instability (due to revolts and threats of depopulation). Affonso found himself subservient not to the Portuguese crown but to the *donatário* of São Tomé upon which the Congo rapidly became dependent. With the situation thus deteriorating in the Congo, King Manuel of Portugal issued a *regimento* or set of instructions and sent a mission to the Congo. The objectives were fourfold: to assist Affonso in the organization of his kingdom; to correct the immoral practices prevalent among priests and other Portuguese who had brought much harm and ill will to the Congo; to better trade relations and assure that Portuguese ships depart from the Congo laden with slaves, ivory, and copper; and to obtain geographical and political knowledge of the area. Although its success was dependent on an allocation of resources far greater than Portugal could give the Congo, the *regimento* did provide a theoretical framework for the projection of European civilization and the establishment of an African protectorate. According to James Duffy, the result was, however, no more than "the frustrated strivings of an African chief, against the opposition of Portuguese freebooters and against a strongly dissident element in his own people, for the attainments of a European culture."

With Affonso's death a struggle for power ensued between a son, Pedro, and a nephew, Diogo. Pedro ruled for several years and then, after a bloody battle, fled to asylum, thus relinquishing his crown. Diogo's reign was to confirm Portuguese lack of interest in adhering to the principle of maintaining an independent Congo (although it theoretically remained independent until 1883). In 1556 the Portuguese in the Congo, envious of the growing commercial importance of Luanda, persuaded Diogo to wage war against the king of neighboring Angola. The Congo force and a Portuguese auxiliary corps were defeated, however, signifying an end to Angola's dependency on the Congo. The dream of Lusitanian assimilation faded as attention turned to Angola. Diogo, a puppet usually subject to the directives of his advisers, was unable to cope with the disruption caused by the slave trade. His death in 1561 precipitated another bitter battle for succession. A civil war ensued, and as the Congo was closed to ships from São Tomé, the slave traffic passed to Angola.

In the late 1560's the Portuguese king, Sebastião, sent reinforcements to the Congo which succeeded in repulsing the Jagas and Anzicos who had invaded the Congo and forced the king and his Portuguese allies to seek refuge on an island in the Congo river. By the end of the sixteenth century, however, not only had Angola eclipsed the Congo, but the latter lapsed into decline as Christian life and the white population gradually disappeared. The Congo began to disintegrate with the emergence of despotic chiefs, marking an end to the Portuguese experiment of assimilating European civilization with African primitive society.

The native African nationalist perspective of the Congo's history differs considerably from interpretation by Portuguese and many other scholars. The African view focuses on his present struggle for independence and on his militant tradition of revolt. To some extent, provincialism and tribalism undercut an emerging consensus that independence implies nationalism for all Angola (former Congolese President Joseph Kasavubu dreamed of a reunited kingdom at the Congo estuary, and the ideals of some leaders of nationalist movements in northern Angola have been challenged as being regionally oriented). There is agreement, however, that inherent in the history of the Congo is a pattern of resistance to the Portuguese presence and influence.

The first evidence of African resistance to a policy of friendship and cooperation with the Portuguese is seen at the end of the fifteenth century in the opposition of Mpanzu a Nzinga to Catholicism and in his apparent success in persuading the king, Nzinga a Nkuwu, to part with his newly acquired religion. Mpanzu, supported by a large army, challenged Affonso I's accession to the throne and lost to a Portuguese-supported military force. But, contend some African nationalists, "Affonso did not have the support of the people." His willingness to cooperate with the Portuguese in their slaving ventures brought internal dissension in the kingdom.

A second instance of resistance is traced to the revolt led by Jorge Muxuebata at Mbanza. Obviously influenced by his missionary advisers, Affonso I ordered all religious idols of the traditional animist cult to be confiscated. The revolt (unsuccessful because of Portuguese aid) therefore was directed at restoration of animist practices as well as at the expulsion of the Portuguese.

In the 1560's there was further evidence of African resistance. With the death of the king, Diogo, the Portuguese residents assassinated the choice of the people and attempted to name their own candidate as king. The people of Mbanza revolted, apparently killing many of the Portuguese. A few years later, about 1570, a popular revolt led by Mbula Matadi was put down by the Congo King, Alvaro I (a stepson of Henrique, the last king of the original dynasty) and his Portuguese allies. At about the same time Portuguese attention turned southward as traders and soldiers joined to embark on the hundred years of Angolan wars and conquest.

In the middle of the seventeenth century, however, the Portuguese moved to destroy the Congo kingdom which had aligned itself with the Dutch during the latter's occupation of Luanda in 1641-48. The Dutch having been expelled, the Portuguese drew up a peace treaty with the Congo, but hostility persisted, a short war was waged, and a final confrontation occurred in October 1665 when a Portuguese force defeated at Ambuíla (Mbwila) the Congo King, António I, and a large army of Africans and a handful of Portuguese residents of the Congo. The death of the king and many of his noblemen was to assure the end of the Congo as a great power, and although the Portuguese could not effectively control the territory (the construction of a fort at Nkoje in 1759 was an unsuccessful attempt to control the slave traffic that flowed through the Congo), they found slave trading possible because of factionalism and disunity among the Congolese provinces.

Formally, the kingdom continued to exist until its unification with Angola and absorption into the present colony in 1883. Absolute Portuguese dominance over the region thereafter was uncertain, however. In 1913 and 1914 Alvaro Tulante Buta led a revolt against the deportation of Congolese laborers to São Tomé. Although this revolt symbolized for Africans their resistance to many centuries of Portuguese rule, the Portuguese maintained a semblance of dynasty and kingdom until the early 1960's.

The Conquest of the Angolan Kingdoms

As Portuguese activity waned in the Congo, attention turned southward to the Mbundu of Ndongo or Angola—the first African nation subject to European colonial rule. The early history of the region is obscured by the conflicting accounts of Cadornega, Cavazzi, and others, yet it is believed that emigrating peoples from central Africa, led by Ngola a Nzinga, invaded the territory south of the Congo and between the Dande and Cuanza rivers, possibly as early as the fourteenth century. The early kingdom, whose capital, Mbanza Kabassa, was located near present-day Dondo, emerged dependent on the Congo whose kings warred and raided among the populous Mbundu and enjoyed prosperity from the sale of captive slaves to the Portuguese. Eventually the wealth and power of the Ngola grew considerable, mainly on the illicit slave trade that filtered through Luanda during the first half of the sixteenth century at a time when the Portuguese government apparently ignored the existence of the Ndongo kingdom.

Flushed with victory over a Congo force in 1556 and having declared his independence of the Congo, the Ngola, probably advised by Portuguese traders from São Tomé, dispatched an emissary to Lisbon, requesting that an official representative be sent to the Ndongo kingdom. This request and the subsequent captivity by the Ngola of that representative, Paulo Dias de Novaes (or Novais), and his Jesuit companions (Balthasar de Castro, who in 1520 led the first official expedition to Ndongo, was held by the Ngola for six years) not only awakened Portuguese interest but provoked eventually a decision to undertake the military conquest of the kingdom. That decision was also conditioned by the Portuguese failure in the Congo, for shortly after news of disaster in the Congo reached Lisbon, the donation charter of 1571 divided Angola into two parts, the section between the Congo border and the Cuanza river being reserved for the crown under Dias' governorship and an area south of the river being given to Dias as hereditary ruler. In return Dias was obligated to settle and provide food and seed (for one year) to one hundred families and to equip and maintain an army of four hundred soldiers and twenty cavalry men as well as build three stone castles.

The new militant policy charging Dias with conquering and colonizing Angola was initiated in 1575. Its principal objectives were the acquisition of land for European settlement, the discovery and control of mineral wealth (especially the silver mines believed to exist in the interior), and the exploitation of the slave trade in order to justify the crown's expenses and effort. Soldiers joined traders in an attempt to fulfill these objectives over the ensuing one hundred years of war with the African kingdoms.

An uneasy peace was shaken in 1578 when a Mbundu chief captured a detachment of eighty Portuguese soldiers, killing twenty of them and returning the others for ransom. A year later, alarmed at a warning that Dias was advancing up the Cuanza, the Ngola (Mbandi Ngola Kiluanje but, among other names, also called Ngola Ndambi and Ngola Mbandi) immediately condemned to death the Portuguese traders at his court and had their goods confiscated. The Ngola then attacked Dias at the fort of Anzele or Nzele, thirty miles inland from Luanda. Although his forces repulsed the attack, the formerly hesitant Dias abandoned all hope for peace and reconciliation, returned to Luanda for reinforcements, and in September 1580 set out with an expeditionary force of three hundred men. Moving up the Cuanza, he first turned upon the independent kingdoms of Kissama (Muxima, Kitangombe, Kizua, Ngola Kikaito, Cafuxe), raiding their villages and recruiting black Africans into an auxiliary army known as the *guerra preta*. Dias reached Makunde in November 1580 but not before the Ngola had driven off a large Congo army of reinforcements. It was therefore three or four years before Dias advanced to the site of

Massangano at the confluence of the Lucala and Cuanza rivers where he defeated the Ngola and established a fort. Thereafter, until his death in 1589, he could do little more than maintain his position at Massangano; at least one subordinate, with a force of one hundred men, was completely routed in an encounter with a neighboring *soba* or chief.

The shift to a militant policy of conquest and the ten years of struggle under Dias marked a first phase in the Angolan wars. The results were disappointing. Dias was able to establish only a few forts along the Cuanza, the Portuguese access to the interior. The wars prevented him from fulfilling the requirement of colonizing the territory. Furthermore, the military ventures suffered from the unexpected loss of thousands of lives, not only from the local wars but from disease. Whereas the slave trade of the past had aroused African suspicions of the Portuguese presence, the military campaigns of conquest had the effect of solidifying and strengthening the African resistance.

The second important phase of the Angolan struggle was characterized by continued Portuguese attempts to implant a colonial system. Dias' successor died soon after attempting to reach the silver mines believed to exist at Cambambe. In 1590 Domingos de Abreu e Brito prepared a detailed report recommending the methodical occupation of Angola, a plan for governing the territory, and the establishment of an overland route between the east and west coasts of Africa. Caught between the entrenched interests of slavers and Jesuits on the one hand and the vacillating policies of the crown on the other, the governor in 1592, Francisco d'Almeida, was unable to carry out that plan nor even reach Cambambe and was forced to leave Angola. Succeeding governors maintained a semblance of peace with the traders, landowners, and Jesuits, but their attempts at occupation of the interior were also without success. The struggle for unity among the Portuguese themselves partially accounted for their early failings in Angola. More important certainly was the established African power against which they were fighting.

The established power was wielded by the kingdom of Ndongo, but that power was partially dependent on the relations between Ndongo and other neighboring Cuanza kingdoms, namely, the Congo, Matamba, Cassanje, and the states of Kissama. In 1590 the Ngola established an alliance with Alvaro II of the Congo and the Jagas of Matamba. The Ngola was also supported by the Imbangala, the marauding invaders who originally emigrated from the Lunda country east of the Cassai river. In December 1590 at Angoleme Aquitambo (Ngoleme a Kitambu) the alliance defeated a Portuguese expedition, which was forced to retreat to Massangano with heavy losses. In April 1594 an African force led by a powerful Kissama chief, Cafuxe Cambara (Kafuche Kabara or Kafushe) ambushed and massacred a Portuguese force at a new fort on the site of the Kissama salt mines, and later other victories were achieved, leaving the Portuguese confined to the unhealthful lowlands and unable to penetrate the plateau country. The Portuguese controlled only a narrow strip stretching between Luanda and the fortress at Massangano but that control was tenuous owing to the unreliability of the native chiefs who professed allegiance to the Portuguese.

A decade of unity allowed the alliance of African kingdoms to withstand the Portuguese advance. About 1600, however, the alliance fell apart as the ravage of the wars brought loss of life and decline in agricultural production. The first sign of disunity occurred with the disaffection of the Jagas of the Matamba kingdom, which lay inland and was less threatened by the Portuguese conquerors. Many Jagas emigrated south to Benguela in search of slaves to be sold to the Portuguese. Others aligned with the Portuguese armies. The Congo kingdom also found itself in a state of disunity as some provinces declared their independence—principally Soyo, whose port at Mpindu controlled the commerce of the Congo river and profited from trade with Europeans, and Dembos which, because of its strategic military and economic importance, benefited from allegiance to the Portuguese. In the kingdom of Ndongo the chiefs Libola and Lucala also abandoned the alliance.

With the disintegration of the African alliance, a Portuguese drive to reach the silver mines of Cambambe met with success in the years 1602 to 1605. No silver was found, shattering the Portuguese dream of many years. The advance to Cambambe and other victories, however, marked the third important phase of the Angolan wars. The successful Portuguese penetration eventually led to the conquest and destruction of the kingdom of Ndongo. In 1603 rebellious chiefs of Kissama, including Cafuxe, were subdued. Shortly thereafter the Ngola was captured and decapitated. The Portuguese continued their offensive, launched a successful campaign in 1616 and 1617, captured the Ndongo capital in 1620, and forced the new king, Ngola Nzinga Mbandi, to seek refuge on an island in the Cuanza. During the next three years the Portuguese exploited the slave trade, depopulating entire communities and devastating the kingdom while still being subject to sporadic attacks by the resistant forces that had rallied about Ngola Nzinga Mbandi.

A fourth phase in the wars was initiated by Mbandi's sister, Nzinga Mbandi (Jinga and later baptized as Anna de Souza Nzinga). In 1621 she went to Luanda as Mbandi's ambassador and negotiated a peace treaty in which the Portuguese agreed to recognize Ndongo as an independent monarchy and to help the Ngola to expel the troublesome Imbangala from Ndongo. The Portuguese did little to rebuild the Ndongo kingdom, however. Mbandi died three years later and was succeeded by Nzinga, who immediately renounced Christianity. The Portuguese policy at this point was not to recognize but to expel the queen and establish a subservient monarchy. The Portuguese governor chose as his puppet, Ari Kiluanje (Samba Ndumbe), a chief of Mpungo a Ndongo (Pungu a Ndong). The inevitable result was renewed war with the Mbundu. Nzinga mobilized her followers and although defeated in her first campaign and forced to withdraw to islands in the Cuanza, she continued attacking the Portuguese and began to build another alliance of African kingdoms. Unable to join together, the Kissama chiefs were defeated by the Portuguese in 1630. About 1631 Dembo Ambuíla, a prestigious chieftain of the Dembos region, revolted against the Portuguese but was subdued by a small Portuguese force allied with a Congolese army under Alvaro IV. By 1635 a new African alliance was achieved, however, this time including, besides Ndongo, the states of Matamba, Congo, Cassanje, Dembos and Kissama.

The emergence of Cassanje and Metamba in the 1630's as powerful kingdoms represented an important shift in the balance of power in Angola. The continuous wars had resulted in the migration of large members of the Imbangala to a position inland, safe from Portuguese attack. Led by Cassanje, these peoples built a new state, which by the end of the seventeenth century became the leading slave-trading kingdom of west central Africa. At the same time the Mbundu abandoned the Ndongo territory and moved northeast and, under Nzinga, conquered the kingdom of Matamba. Realizing the loss of slave commerce in the depopulated Ndongo, the Portuguese turned to the distant Cassanje and Matamba kingdoms for slaves. Having failed to negotiate peacefully with the kingdoms, the Portuguese resorted to military conquest. However, when the Dutch captured Luanda in 1641, the Portuguese found themselves confined to Massangano, challenged on two fronts. In 1643 a Portuguese force was surprised, and two hundred soldiers were taken prisoner. Two years later a relief army was overwhelmed. However, the Portuguese established a *modus vivendi* with the Dutch, who provided food and supplies in exchange for slaves. As a result, states David Birmingham, the Portuguese "had sunk from being masters of the slave trade to being its most servile participants. The capture and sale of slaves became vital not only to their prosperity but to their very survival."

The Portuguese position was strengthened by the arrival in 1648 of the new governor, Salvador Correia de Sá and a force from Rio de Janeiro which succeeded in expelling the Dutch and then attempted to reestablish and consolidate Portuguese authority in the territory. Thus commenced the fifth and final phase of the hundred years of Angolan wars. The defeat of the Dutch coincided with the breakup of the African coalition; for in 1647 the Cassanje kingdom, desirous of promoting the slave trade, aligned itself with Portugal. A year later the Congo king signed a treaty of peace with Correia de Sá, although hostility continued until a confrontation in October 1665 at Mbwila, where the Congolese army was completely destroyed.

An accord with Nzinga's Matamba kingdom was reached in 1656, and she maintained commercial ties with the Portuguese until her death seven years later. The agreement prompted dissent from the son and successor to Ngola Ari of Ndongo, who planned to reestablish Ndongo as a powerful kingdom. The matter was resolved in 1671 by the last of wars between the Portuguese and Ndongo. The Portuguese attacked the Ngola's capital, killing the Ngola in battle and capturing many of his subjects as slaves. This event marked the effective end of the Ndongo kingdom.

Matamba remained a problem. There, after a long struggle for control, Ngola Kanini emerged a powerful leader. Assisted to power by the Portuguese, Kanini eventually turned against them and also against their trading ally, the kingdom of Cassanje, which he plundered and destroyed. Subsequently, Kanini defeated a Portuguese military force at Katole, and only his death and Matamba's need for establishing trade links provided Portugal with a solution to the situation. A peace treaty was signed in 1683. Peace reigned only a half century, however, and Matamba as well as Cassanje continued as intermediaries to dominate the trade that filtered from the eastern Lunda and Holo states to the Portuguese markets. Portuguese attempts to bypass Matamba and Cassanje were futile, even after their invasion, launched in 1744, had advanced them to the capital of Matamba. The Portuguese withdrew, and Matamba continued its trade dominance as well as commercial relations with Portugal's European rivals.

From the early nineteenth century until about 1850, the Portuguese reestablished themselves as the principal slave traders of the Angolan coast. Their success was attributed to the continued use of the African auxiliary units or *guerra preta*, to taxation practices, and to the treaties and oral agreements made with the native *sobas*. At the same time, foreign competition declined with the enactment of anti-slavery legislation, legislation which also affected the Portuguese slave trade in the late nineteenth century. [In his detailed study Douglas Wheeler divides this period into the initial expansion (1836-1861) coinciding with the gradual abolition of slavery; the withdrawal and concentration along the coast (1861-1877); and the penetration to the Bié plateau (1877-1891).]

African hostility continued to be as strong as three centuries earlier, however. The Dembos region, northwest of Luanda, persistently resisted Portuguese expeditions sent to the interior and was especially troublesome after 1850. War broke out in 1872, but only after military campaigns of 1907 and 1908 could the Portuguese claim effective occupation of the region. Complete pacification and access to the Congo frontier were achieved with the Dembos military operations of 1918 and 1919.

The Benguela Highlands and the Native Resistance to the South

In the late sixteenth century the Portuguese began to carry on trade with the coastal peoples south of the Cuanza. About 1584 they established a fortress at Benguela a Velha (Pôrto Amboim) and about 1617 founded a permanent settlement at Benguela a Nova or São Felipe de Benguela. Throughout the century, until the building of a presidio at Caconda on the edge of the Bié plateau about 1580, the Portuguese launched several exploratory expeditions inland from Benguela. The first presidio was destroyed by the soba Bongo in 1684 and rebuilt nearly a year later (a third at Caconda Nova was built in 1769). From the late seventeenth century onwards, the Portuguese began to penetrate the kingdoms of the plateau. Their immediate objective, as in Angola, was the discovery of minerals, especially copper, which was not found. Instead the flow of slaves from Benguela increased, and by the end of the eighteenth century the colony achieved some importance.

Many African kingdoms of the Ovimbundu resisted the Portuguese attempts to penetrate the interior. Among these kingdoms were the Huambo (Huamba, Hambo or Wambo), probably established early in the seventeenth century at the present site of Nova Lisboa; Tchiyaka, founded to the west of Huambo about 1650; Ndulu, located about 1671 in the region known today as Andulo; Bailundo, founded by the chief Katiavala perhaps as early as 1700; Bié (Bihé or Viyé), established about 1750 by Viyé, an elephant hunter of the Humbe people to the south; and Caconda (Kakonda), founded by an African with the same name about 1760.

Organized resistance to the Portuguese advance was evident as early as 1660 when the king of Tchiyaka, Kapango I, forced the withdrawal of a Portuguese expedition which had attempted to reach the plateau. In 1698 the *soba* of Huambo failed in an attempt to expel the Portuguese, although in 1718 a coalition of kingdoms, led by Tchiyaka, successfully attacked the fortress at Caconda, necessitating temporarily a Portuguese withdrawal from the region. A half century later the Portuguese invaded the kingdom of Galangue (Ngalangi), seizing the king and at the same time establishing an alliance with the king of Caconda who allowed them to construct a new fortress.

The new presidio at Caconda was established to protect existing trade and to stimulate new trade with the interior kingdoms. Much of the trade was carried on by soldiers of the military expeditions which occasionally ventured inland. Gradually the hinterlands opened to all traders, although beyond the range of the guns of the presidios, the Europeans found themselves subject to the wishes of a native king to whom they often were forced to pay tribute. The intrusion of the trader into the life of the African native inevitably provoked tension and conflict leading to further wars. Such a war was that of 1774-1776, at which time the Portuguese invaded the kingdoms of Tchiyaka, Ndulu, and Bailundo in order to dominate the commercial activity of the region. During the two-year campaign the Portuguese achieved their objective of conquering the kingdoms but failed to maintain effective occupation. The kingdoms therefore continued their independence from Portuguese control.

Until 1778 the Portuguese campaign had little impact upon the kingdom of Bié, which prospered from commercial ties not only with the Portuguese but with the Lunda and the Makakolo tribes that had reached the upper Zambeze. In 1778, however, Kangombe, with the support of the Portuguese, dethroned the reigning king and established an alliance with Portugal (effective until the late nineteenth century). As a result Bié, which also benefited from its central location, quickly emerged as the commercial center of the plateau.

As Bié and also Bailundo dominated trade with the Portuguese, other kingdoms of the plateau found themselves competitively disadvantaged and resorted to raiding, plunder, and warfare. By the nineteenth century the plateau had experienced anarchy and unequal growth among the kingdoms and had more and more found itself subservient to trade conditions imposed by the Portuguese while experiencing a partial disintegration of traditional patterns of indigenous productivity, especially in handicrafts.

The ascension to power of Ekuikui II of Bailundo brought a temporary halt to the disintegration of the traditional Ovimbundu order and also to the region's impending loss of independence. The astute king concentrated on developing agriculture and artisan crafts as well as the lucrative rubber trade with the Portuguese. As Bailundo prospered, Ekuikui sought an alliance with Bié and persuaded the king, Tchyoka, to abandon his ally, the Portuguese. Tchyoka broke that traditional tie in 1886, prompting the Portuguese to begin a campaign of encirclement of the two kingdoms.

First, the Portuguese conquered the kingdom of Galangue and established a fort at Cubango. Two years later Tchyoka died, and his successor, Ndunduma I (Chindunduma or Cikunyu), joined with Ekuikui II to impose limitations upon Portuguese labor practices in particular but also on commercial relations. A large Portuguese punitive column of regular troops and auxiliaries then moved against Bié, which succumbed about 1890. Ndunduma, persuaded to surrender, was exiled to the Cape Verde islands. The Portuguese occupied Bailundo about the same time. An era of relatively independent existence ended for the two kingdoms, although Ekuikui's successor, Numa II, attacked the fort established to control the region and died in battle in 1896.

After 1890 European traders settled in Bié and Bailundo in ever increasing numbers. Their desire for land and contract labor brought friction and, along with abuses by military and administrative officials, eventually encouraged a native revolt. In 1902 the Bailundo king, Mutu-ya-Kevela, led dissident Africans in rebellion. An attempt was made to recover land held by the Europeans, and the Bailundo area was swept by a wave of murder, looting, and destruction of trading posts. A Portuguese column of several hundred men quickly retaliated, first defeating the rebels near Nova Lisboa and later subduing all Bailundo and Bié by burning African villages and overcoming scattered resistance. A year later peace had been restored throughout the kingdoms of the Ovimbundu, although an area northwest of Nova Lisboa continued open hostility to the Portuguese well into 1904.

Portuguese attempts to penetrate the interior also were evidenced in the region south of the kingdoms of the Ovimbundu. Since the late sixteenth century that region had been dominated by the kingdoms of Huíla and Humbe. The former was the most important and powerful and until the late eighteenth century controlled an area stretching from the coast to the Cunene river, while Humbe reigned over a smaller area eastward from the Cunene. After the death in 1787 of its king, Kanina, Huíla splintered into several independent states. Humbe also subdivided into several kingdoms.

Tribal disunity resulted from increasing Portuguese activity in the region. A serious effort at occupying Huíla was attempted about 1769 when a European colony was established at Salvaterra de Magos. Although division within the kingdom made occupation less difficult, the Portuguese encountered African resistance throughout the nineteenth century. Attacking Portuguese forts and settlements in Huíla, invading forces from the kingdoms of the Ovimbundu launched the "Nano Wars." The initial thrust of the African invasion was at Salvaterra de Magos in 1803, 1804, and 1806. A second phase involved African clashes against the Portuguese garrison of Huíla in 1832, 1838, 1848, 1849, 1857, 1860, and 1879.

In Humbe, African resistance began about 1858 when an uprising resulted in a temporary expulsion of the Portuguese. Although a fortress was built by 1880, intermittent revolts manifested African hostility. Near the turn of the century a disease from South-West Africa infected the cattle of the area, and a Portuguese detachment was sent to convince the African population that their cattle should be vaccinated. They refused and massacred the soldiers. The Portuguese sent a small army to quell the disorder. In 1904, however, the Cuanhama people of the region ambushed a Portuguese force encamped at Cuamato, killing three hundred. Although two thousand troops overwhelmed the Cuanhama rebels in 1906, resistance, partially supported by Germans in South-West Africa, continued until a major campaign in 1915 assured fortification and control of the area.

Nationalist Rebellion in the 1960's

Warfare between the Portuguese and the tribes of Angola had gone on sporadically since the late fifteenth century. Ultimate occupation and pacification of the colony, however, was attempted during a half century of military campaigns launched during the last third of the nineteenth century. Those campaigns, described in much of the available literature as heroic struggles for the Portuguese cause, began and ended in the Dembos region. With the outbreak in 1872 of war by Dembos chiefs residing less than a hundred miles from Luanda, the African acknowledged that the hundred years of wars for conquest of the Angolan kingdoms had not relegated him forever to a subservient role. To quell African unrest in the former Angolan kingdoms east of Luanda, Portuguese military expeditions were carried out at Dembos in 1907-1908 and 1918-1919; near Moxico in 1895, 1903, and 1912; and in Lunda in 1896, 1900, and 1906-1907. Portuguese activity in the Congo included operations during 1874, 1887, 1892-1893, 1896, 1900-1901, 1908, 1914, and 1916. Major campaigns in the kingdoms of the Ovimbundu occurred at Cubango in 1885-1896 and 1909; in Bailundo during 1888 and 1902-1903; in Bié during 1890 and Novo Redondo during 1893 and 1903-1904; and at Caconda in 1903.

In the Humbe-Huíla region Portuguese military activities were conspicuous in 1885-1886, 1891, 1893, 1897-1898, 1902, 1904-1907, and 1914-1915.

Portuguese containment of the African resistance and hostility was not assured by the turn of the century, as evidenced first by the Bailundo revolt and later by the Cuamato disaster, the uprisings at Dembos, the 1913 rebellion of Tulante Buta in the Portuguese Congo, and revolts in Pôrto Amboim in 1917 and 1924. An uprising in Ambriz a year later and in Cubal in 1940, along with occasional workers' strikes, were clear indicators of discontent in the colony.

During the 1950's, reports of African protest and Portuguese suppression were more frequent, especially after the Portuguese secret police extended its operations to Angola. The major incidents involved the arrest and deportation during February 1956 of three African leaders to a prison camp in Bié and the arrests of hundreds of nationalist suspects on March 29, 1959, as well as the imprisonment in Luanda of 150 Africans during July and additional arrests in the autumn. In December 50 Angolans and seven Europeans were indicted for crimes against Portugal, and within a year all were tried secretly and sentenced to imprisonment. Police containment of African political activity was evidenced especially after the 1958 electoral campaign when manifestoes and programs demanded independence.

In June 1960 the Movimento Popular de Libertação de Angola (MPLA) sent a memorandum to the Portuguese government, requesting a peaceful solution to the colonial question. Ignoring the request, the Portuguese arrested 52 persons throughout Angola, including Agostinho Neto, a poet and MPLA leader, and Joaquim Pinto de Andrade, a Catholic priest. When villagers from Neto's region east of Luanda went to Catete to demand his release, they were met by troops who fired upon them, killing about thirty and wounding others. In July Portuguese troops reportedly engaged in "terror raids" in Luanda. On September 3, the MPLA issued an appeal to the United Nations to discuss the Angolan situation, and in a December meeting with other nationalist organizations in London the MPLA warned that the Portuguese government had ignored all efforts at negotiation and was preparing to wage war against Angolans.

These developments were a prelude to the violent struggle that began in early 1961. In the Malange district during January and February a large number of cotton workers were reported to have protested against low wages and working conditions. Their demonstrations provoked severe Portuguese reprisals, including the bombing of many villages and the killing of a substantial number of Africans. Dissatisfaction with Portuguese rule and repression probably provoked popular support for the unsuccessful attacks during February 4-6 on a Luanda prison, radio station, and military barracks, although leadership for the uprising was partially provided by MPLA adherents in Luanda.

In mid-March another nationalist organization, the União das Populações de Angola (UPA) led a rebellion in the North, apparently after laborers on the Primavera coffee plantation near São Salvador approached their employer for pay. The employer insulted the laborers, killed several, and then was overwhelmed by Africans who armed themselves with sticks, stones, and gasoline and attacked every European house in the vicinity. From São Salvador the uprising spread across the Portuguese Congo, then south to the Malange and Luanda districts and later to Nova Lisboa. Portuguese military forces, caught by surprise, withdrew from forts at Maquela and Quibaxe, thereby exposing northern Angola to military occupation by the UPA forces. Although the initial outbreak at Primavera appears to have been spontaneous, the UPA claimed credit for the rebellion, stating that it had not only circulated manifestoes calling for a general uprising on March 15 but had organized many strikes among plantation workers in northern Angola during preceding months.

At first the Portuguese were disorganized. A few sorties were made into African villages where, according to surviving refugees, the population was shot down. Unconfirmed reports estimated that twenty thousand Africans were killed by the "systematic repression" that followed in late March and April. According to refugee reports, Portuguese planes strafed and dropped napalm bombs on small villages and fleeing Africans. By late April Portugal employed emergency measures to deal with the situation. The UPA army, utilizing traditional warfare and suffering heavy casualties in the face of vastly superior arms of the Portuguese forces, adopted guerrilla tactics. The Angolan nationalist forces were hindered by the arrival of the dry season in May, for the Portuguese announced that their tactic would be the burning of the tall grass in which Africans were hiding and the encirclement of nationalist forces to cut off supplies and communication with the leaders in Léopoldville. At the same time the Portuguese encouraged tribal rivalry by using African troops from the south, and a voluntary corps of Africans was established as an auxiliary organization of the armed forces whose task was to harvest the valuable coffee crop of the north. Also "psycho-social" units were employed in an attempt to lure back the rebels and refugees by persuading them that the army was their protector. By July the Portuguese had checked the rebellion on a line running roughly from Luanda through Salazar to Forte República, near the Congo border. North of this line the Portuguese extended their hold to a few villages and towns. In August, Portuguese forces recaptured Nambuangongo, a strategic point in their drive to reoccupy the north. In October the governor general announced that the war had ended, the enemy was dispersed, and all villages and administrative posts were reoccupied.

In December, however, the MPLA declared it was ready to take the offensive. At the same time the UPA announced that Angolans were being trained in Algeria and that a provisional government would be established. A Governo Revolucionário de Angola em Exílio (GRAE) was formally proclaimed in April 1962, and in August a military camp for Angolans was established in Congo territory.

Despite these developments, the nationalists found themselves not only confronted by overwhelming Portuguese military armaments and manpower but also beset by serious internal dissension, first between the MPLA and the UPA, later among dissident factions in each organization. From late 1962 until early 1966 the nationalist struggle to end colonialism was obscured by factionalism and personal struggles for control of the movement. One explanation for this erratic behavior is found through examination of the organizational growth of Angolan nationalism during the present century as well as certain geographic and cultural-social considerations that differentiate the principal African movements.

The African resistance and occasional protests by liberal Portuguese Angolans, who in the late nineteenth century demanded abolition of slavery and forced labor and a national culture for the colony, constituted the roots of nationalist sentiment which later expressed itself in several organizations. A Partido Pro-Angola was formed in the early 1920's and advocated a program of administrative autonomy for Angola. The Liga Nacional Africana (LNA), established by white settlers in 1929, limited itself to demands for reforms to be achieved through legal processes. In the 1940's, after mulattoes and Negroes had been admitted as members, there was division in the LNA's ranks over the issue of righting grievances by encouraging the direct participation of the African masses. In 1956 the Liga issued a manifesto deploring the plight of the African and a year later declined a Portuguese request to send a delegation to the United Nations in support of the claim that Angola was an integral part of the mother country. As a result the governor general intervened and replaced the elected leadership with administrative committees. Another organization founded in 1929, the Grêmio Africano, later became the Associação

Regional dos Naturais de Angola. Comprised of African intellectuals from Luanda, it advocated mass African participation and carried out its struggle against "repressive colonialism" by clandestine and semiclandestine means. Other organizations included the Associação Africana do Sul de Angola, which was founded about 1954 by railway workers of Nova Lisboa and suppressed soon after for its militant orientation; *Avante*, a youth group of Bié which was censured by Portuguese authorities in the early 1950's; and numerous voluntary African sports and religious groups. As an outgrowth of the early organizational activity, two African cultural magazines briefly appeared: A *Mensagem*, edited by Viriato da Cruz, and A *Cultura*.

Official Portuguese sources allege that early nationalist activity among black Africans was promoted by three secret and autonomous organizations established about 1948: the Comité Federal Angolano do Partido Comunista Português, the Comissão de Luta das Juventudes contra o Imperialismo Colonial em Angola, and Angola Negra. In early 1952 an attempt was made to unify the underground organizations into a Conselho de Libertação de Angola. By October 1955 a small Partido Comunista Angolano (PCA) was active clandestinely in Luanda, Catete, and Malange.

Nationalist sources contend, however, that Angola's first revolutionary party was the Partido da Luta Unida dos Africanos de Angola (PLUA), established in 1953 by Viriato da Cruz. Its first manifesto exhorted Africans to join underground groups and unite in a broad movement for the liberation of the colony. Although Portuguese authorities insist that the PLUA functioned as a Communist front organization, the PCA apparently dissolved when the PLUA and other organizations formed the MPLA in December 1956, and Viriato da Cruz was named secretary general. The MPLA emerged as an indigenous nationalist movement engaged in continual agitation while issuing leaflets setting forth its policy. At the same time it created underground schools for illiterates. After the arrest of several of its leaders in late March 1959, the MPLA decided to carry on its work in exile at Conakry, where it remained until October 1961, when it transferred headquarters to Léopoldville.

The MPLA tactic of the united front which marked its origin was applied with the establishment of coalitions of nationalist parties from all the Portuguese colonies, the first being formed at Tunis during January 1960 and the second at Rabat in April 1961. The tactic was also utilized during a desperate leadership crisis and party split in July 1963. At that time Viriato da Cruz denounced MPLA president Agostinho Neto for collaboration with the Portuguese (Neto, held since June 1959, had mysteriously escaped from a prison in Portugal in 1962). Cruz established a provisional executive committee to run the party but later proclaimed his support for the MPLA's rival, the Frente Nacional de Libertação de Angola (FNLA —a coalition including the UPA) and for the GRAE led by Holden Roberto. At the time, the African Liberation Committee of the Organization of African Unity (OAU) favored giving technical and material assistance to Roberto's movement. Meanwhile, Neto announced the formation of a Frente Democrática para a Libertação de Angola (FDLA) which grouped together the MPLA with four smaller organizations, all of which promptly split, with one faction remaining with the FDLA and the other declaring itself either independent of the FDLA or desirous of adhering to the FNLA. Neto announced that the FDLA wished to join the GRAE (but not the FNLA) to give it "representative character." Neto's offer was refused by Roberto, who then accepted the FNLA membership bids of Cruz and others. Mário de Andrade, an intellectual and poet who until Neto's return to Léopoldville had served the MPLA as acting president, refused to respond to claims made by both MPLA factions that he supported them and temporarily withdrew from the MPLA until mid-1965 by which time Neto had reconstituted his movement in Brazzaville.

The MPLA following comes from the discontented "assimilated" mulatto elite of the Angolan cities. Granted citizenship, this elite had access to education denied most black Africans. Although it opposed the Salazar dictatorship, the MPLA, whose membership and support included some white Portuguese, at first assumed an ambivalent position on national independence for Angola. Without doubt its role in the abortive uprising in Luanda during early February 1961 foreshadowed the rebellion throughout northern Angola, yet that important event seems to have been connected in some degree with the Portuguese opposition's seizure of the liner "Santa Maria" a month earlier. From 1961 until its split in 1963 the MPLA engaged in little military activity, for the myth of its involvement in the Angolan war was exposed by Cruz in hearings before the African Liberation Committee which eventually endorsed Roberto's exile government as the only effective nationalist movement fighting for Angolan independence. Subsequently Roberto's movement experienced a series of internal crises, and the OAU decision was modified to aid a revitalized MPLA which, under Neto's leadership, recognized its earlier mistakes and reoriented itself toward the revolutionary struggle.

Roberto's FNLA was a coalition, formed in March 1962, of the UPA and the Partido Democrático de Angola (PDA), the latter led by Emmanuel Kounzika and formerly known as the Aliança Zombo (Aliazo) comprised of Bazombo emigrés living in the former Belgian Congo. In 1958 Roberto emerged as president of the UPA, a reorganized version of the União das Populações do Norte de Angola (UPNA) which he had helped found during 1954; but subsequently he disassociated himself from the original leadership over the issue of restoring the Bacongo kingdom. As a regionally oriented movement, the UPNA apparently evolved after Protestant Angolans in the Congo failed in an attempt to have their nominee, Manuel Barros Nekaka, uncle of Holden Roberto, named successor to the old Congo monarchy. With Portuguese support, the candidate of rival Catholics living in Angola was named king. António's reign was brief, as was that of his wife Isabel. The Catholic movement supporting the monarchy evolved into a rival political party, Ngwizako-Ngwizani a Kongo, about 1960 with headquarters in Léopoldville. Apparently in September 1962 the Portuguese decided to revive the monarchy and named Pedro VIII as king. He died a month later.

Roberto structured the UPA and later the FNLA as a mass revolutionary party with a highly centralized organization. A central committee represented the party throughout the administrative units of Angola while decision-making power rested with Roberto as chairman of a political bureau of five men appointed by him. Roberto also served as commander-in-chief of his army. His mass party incorporated organizations of youth, labor, and women. At the height of its success during 1961-1963 the party claimed a dues-paying membership of forty thousand, largely among the large Angolan population in Léopoldville and thousands of sympathizers in northern Angola, while the ranks of its poorly equipped army may have reached fifteen thousand soldiers.

Roberto's movement represented the peasant masses of Angolan émigrés and refugees in the Congo as well as supporters in northern Angola. At first, attempts were made to include a balance of Angolans of all ethnic groups as leaders in the provisional government and officers in the army. By 1964, however, it was clear that no such balance would be achieved, for the party and army leadership remained predominantly drawn from Roberto's Quicongo-speaking peoples of northern Angola and especially the Congo itself. This regional and tribal orientation was made more apparent by defections beginning in 1962 when Roberto's first military commander, Marcos Cassanga, resigned his post. His replacement, José Kalundungo (a representative of the Ovimbundu of the south) resigned in mid-1964 and at the same time denounced Roberto for disrupting the army, using the base at Kinkouzou for propaganda and not for military training, and purging and assassinating dissident comrades. On July 16,

1964, the minister of foreign affairs, Jonas Savimbi (also from the south), resigned and denounced Roberto for nepotism and for favoring the Bacongo tribe of northern Angola (at the time twelve of the nineteen ministry posts were held by Bacongos, of whom seven were Roberto's blood relatives). A week later José Liahuca, medical director of the government's refugee relief organization, also resigned. On the night of June 24 and 25, 1965, defense minister Alexandre Taty joined with Andrés Kassinda, ransacked, and briefly occupied the headquarters in Léopoldville. According to Roberto, Kassinda and Taty were aided by Congolese police and also were working as agents of the Portuguese secret police.

Although recognized by many nations, Roberto's provisional government was vulnerable to charges levied on several fronts. Its rival, the MPLA, dismissed it as a regional faction. The Portuguese concurred in this view, insisting that the uprising affected only a small part of the territory and was not representative of national discontent. The Protestant orientation of Roberto and his colleagues also bolstered the Portuguese contention that Protestant missionaries were to blame for the revolt. Roberto's success was partially dependent on relations with the Congo government. His apparent rejection of former President Joseph Kasavubu's conception of a Bacongo state encompassing the lower Congo region and northern Angola resulted in strained relations and led to police harassment of the activities of the GRAE, especially during 1964 and 1965. Earlier, Roberto's friendship with Congolese prime ministers Patrice Lumumba and especially Cyrille Adoulla brought him support.

By 1966 the nationalist struggle had reached an impasse. Roberto's movement, weakened by defections and lack of financial support, was prevented by the Congolese from pursuing a policy of militant action. The MPLA intelligentsia continued its long-range political and economic planning while claiming military success in the enclave of Cabinda. In March the provisional government accused the MPLA of torturing and killing Matias Migueis and José Miguel, supporters of Viriato da Cruz who had defected from the MPLA in July 1963. Meanwhile, increasing numbers of splinter groups petitioned the United Nations, the Congo governments, and even the Portuguese for support of their activities. At the same time a wave of military coups against revolutionary governments in Ghana and elsewhere in Africa seemed to convince Portuguese authorities that nationalism had reached an impasse in independent Africa and that the time would come when international opinion and a majority of Africans would accept Portuguese rule in Angola and the other colonies.

FIVE

PORTUGUESE GUINÉ,

THE CAPE VERDE ARCHIPELAGO,

AND SÃO TOMÉ AND PRÍNCIPE

In 1953 Portuguese police allegedly massacred an estimated one thousand native Africans on the island of São Tomé. Ten years later a military official acknowledged that fifteen per cent of the territory of Guiné had fallen to the control of African insurgents. The interim decade represented a phase of incipient nationalism in which African leaders searched for a new identity and new ideals. At the same time they demanded developmental solutions for their long-neglected territories, an end to colonialism, and independence allowing for national integration and an end to tribal divisions that historically had impeded their sporadic yet continuing resistance to the Portuguese presence.

Situated on the west coast of Africa between Senegal and the Republic of Guinée, Portuguese Guiné, roughly two-fifths the size of Portugal, forms a triangular enclave comprising a mainland, the Bijagós archipelago, and a string of coastal islands including Bolama, Pecixe, Jata, and many others. Lacking good natural boundaries and lying in a zone of rainy tropical climate, the greater part of Portuguese Guiné is lowland, much of it periodically inundated by tidal waters, that in few places exceeds several hundred feet above sea level.

In these alluvial districts much of the soil is rich in humus and is particularly fertile where well drained. Less productive laterite soils are found near the swampy coast and on the flood plains of many rivers. Along the greatly indented coast, stretching from Cape Roxo to Cajete Point, are the chief ports of Cacheu on the river of the same name; Bissau, the largest port, on the estuary of the Gêba; Teixeira Pinto on the Mansôa; and Bolama on the island of Bolama. In the important river system, the Cacheu winds more than two hundred miles to the east central part of the country; it is navigable to the town of Farim. The Gêba rises in Senegal, flows southwest, and is navigable from Bafatá to the sea. Its principal tributary, the Colufe, enters on the left bank near Bafatá. The Rio Grande

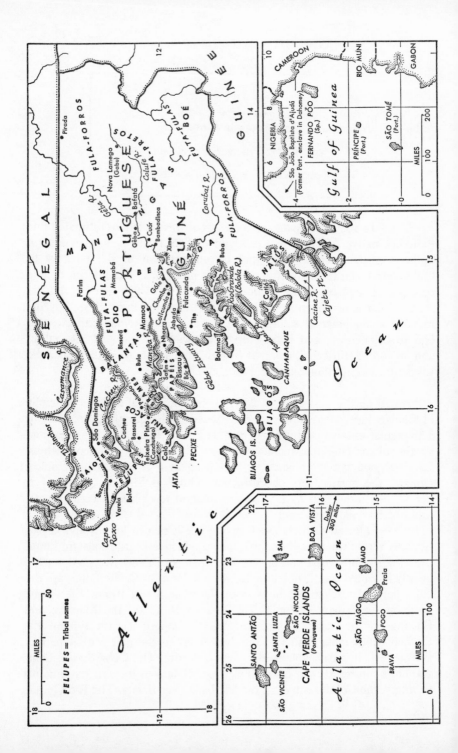

or Bolola and the Corubal also flow into the Gêba. Other rivers are the Mansôa between the Gêba and the Cacheu, the Tombali, and the Cacine near the southern border.

According to the 1950 census, less than two per cent of Guiné's half million inhabitants were classified as "civilized." Only some two thousand were Europeans, a figure that has been substantially augmented by thousands of Portuguese soldiers sent to the colony in recent years to quell the nationalist rebellion. Most of the "civilized" population is distributed among the cities of Bissau, the capital since 1941, and Bolama, the old capital, and the townships of Bafatá, Farim, Teixeira Pinto, Mansôa, Nova Lamego, Catió, and Bissorã. The *lingua franca* is a Portuguese creole highly influenced by Cape Verdean dialects and indigenous languages. Less than two per cent of the population is literate, and government funds for educational facilities and teachers are inadequate. The few Catholic missions have the responsibility for education of the Africans. Some districts are without schools altogether, although scattered throughout the territory are some five hundred Muslim elementary (and mainly religious) schools with low standards. Poor health conditions affect most of the population, the major diseases being malaria, tuberculosis, trachoma, and parasitic infections.

The crescent-shaped archipelago of the ten Cape Verde islands lying off the west coast of Africa was uninhabited until the Portuguese first arrived in the fifteenth century. With the immigration of families from southern Portugal and the recruitment of African workers from the continent, mainly from Portuguese Guiné, the population by 1960 amounted to two hundred thousand. Because the Cape Verde islands were first settled by the Portuguese, they officially have a culture different from and superior to mainland Africa, and therefore the inhabitants are "civilized" Portuguese citizens. They speak a creole Portuguese and have their own literature and characteristic songs, called *mournas*. They are known for their intellectual aspirations and, in fact, have greater access to education than do Guineans, Angolans, and Moçambicans, although the illiteracy rate may be as high as eighty per cent. Mulattoes or creoles comprise the majority of the population, but there are also important European and African minorities. The racial integration of several centuries lends apparent support to Lusotropical theory. The early settlers recklessly destroyed the forests to clear ground for their plantations, with the result that the storms carry away more and more of the loose, treeless soil. Droughts and famines have from time to time brought death to tens of thousands of inhabitants.

São Tomé and Príncipe islands constitute an overseas province lying in the Gulf of Guiné off the west coast of Africa. The islands, appearing as a maze of mountains cut by deep ravines, have a population of more than sixty thousand, largely mixed and of Portuguese and African origins; this population is supplemented by recruited labor from other Portuguese territories in Africa. Scattered on the cocoa plantations and estates, the indigenous population speaks a Portuguese creole while the Angolares (descendants of Angolan slaves shipwrecked in the sixteenth century) retain their old forms of speech. Traditionally most of the inhabitants have been classified as Portuguese citizens, although a third of the population was listed as unassimilated in the 1950 census. Illiteracy is high, owing to inadequate educational facilities.

An isolated settlement in Dahomey, São João Baptista d'Ajudá, was incorporated into the province of São Tomé and Príncipe in 1680. It was evacuated but reoccupied by the Portuguese in 1844. However, the Portuguese withdrew from the Dahomey coast in 1887, and five years later the French annexed Ajudá and other districts. Thereafter until 1961 the Portuguese claimed the fort of Ajudá as an administrative dependency of São Tomé and Príncipe. Six hours after the government of Dahomey reannexed the enclave in 1961 the Portuguese resident at Ajudá fled, setting fire to the fort and leaving it in ruins.

The Historical Perspective

Having failed after the capture of Ceuta in 1415 to oust the Arabs from Morocco, the Portuguese under the leadership of Prince Henry the Navigator systematically explored the west coast of Africa. The Portuguese were the first Europeans to sail along the coast south of Cape Bojador, rounded by Gil Eanes in 1434. A decade later the mouth of the Senegal was reached, and about 1445 Nuno Tristão passed beyond Cape Verde to Guiné ("Guiné" being a European word derived from Arabic and meaning "land of black men"). The opening up of the coastal zone was followed by expeditions to the interior, up the Gambia, Rio Grande, and other rivers, and overland to the interior African kingdoms.

The period of history from 1434 until 1550 may be named that of discovery and exploration. The Cape Verde islands were discovered before 1460, probably by an Italian navigator, Antonio de Noli, although the exact date is confused by the conflicting chronicles of Alvise Cà da Mosta (Luís da Cadamosto) and Diogo Gomes. A decade or two later São Tomé and adjacent islands were discovered. The purpose of exploration, according to the chronicler, Azurara, was to divert the control of west African trade from Muslim to Portuguese merchants and to find Christian allies to overcome Islam. To accomplish this, fortresses were established at strategic points: at Arguim, in Upper Guiné, which fell into decline as the Portuguese found easier trade to the south; at Cacheu on the estuary of the river with the same name in present day Guiné; and at São Jorge da Mina (Elmina), Axim, Shama, and Accra along the Gold Coast.

The key links to Portuguese control over Western Africa were the Cape Verde archipelago and São Tomé. In the 1460's the Cape Verdes, São Tiago island in particular, were colonized and developed into a base for trade in slaves and other commodities with the adjacent mainland. Special privileges and rights were given to the Cape Verde settlers, who easily obtained slaves from the neighboring African coast. This Cape Verde hegemony over the Guiné coast contributed to its widespread exploitation and abuse and the development of a half-caste society that attracted to it undesirable European fugitives and exiles. The result was a deterioration of Portuguese influence, which the government unsuccessfully attempted to check in the early fifteenth century by revoking the mainland trading rights of the Cape Verdeans and by supporting Catholic missionaries from Portugal. São Tomé also became important to the Portuguese trade, particularly as a depot for slaves bound for Brazil. Portuguese sugar plantations worked by African slaves brought great prosperity to Sáo Tomé until about 1570 when planters began to transfer their activities to tropical Brazil.

Throughout the latter half of the sixteenth century and all of the seventeenth, the Portuguese in Guiné experienced a period of declining influence and increasing challenge from foreign interests, although the slave trade filtering through Cacheu and Bissau increased greatly. Individual French and English expeditions ventured to western Africa, but throughout most of the sixteenth century Portugal was the only European nation to maintain control on west African soil. However, the defeat at Alcácer-Kebir resulting in the incorporation of Portugal and her dominions by the Spanish crown in 1580 all but foreshadowed the eclipse of Portuguese power and sovereignty in most of West Africa. In 1637 the Dutch captured São Jorge da Mina and Arguim a year later, although they were beaten off at Cacheu and in the islands.

The foreign challenge to Portuguese rule in Africa was accompanied by poor economic organization resulting from administrative centralization and intervention by the Crown. Portuguese outlaws, or lançados, living in the bush illegally supplied foreign competitors with goods, thereby undermining Portugal's economic control. Nevertheless these lançados and their mulatto descendants called filhos da terra worked closely with Christianized Africans known as *grumetes* and helped Portugal to maintain its hold on the territory of Guiné. Portugal's continued presence was also protected by the neighboring Cape Verdes and the rebuilding of the fortress at Bissau during the seventeenth and eighteenth centuries and further assured by the Dutch failure to capture Cacheu.

An administrator, Honório Pereira Barreto, distinguished himself during the period 1837-1859. Barreto stabilized finance, acquired new territories, settled many Cape Verdeans and Portuguese, and brought to the long neglected colony a short period of recovery. Guiné languished, however, with the suppression of the slave trade, increased foreign competition for commodity markets, and poor agricultural production. Portuguese prestige was further lowered by the inability to defend against the ever-increasing attacks of the native tribes.

The British and French again threatened Portuguese interests toward the end of the nineteenth century. Unstable political conditions had led to neglect of colonial matters during the early part of the century, permitting the French to occupy Casamance, and attempts were made to occupy Bissau and Cacheu. These encroachments were accompanied by British colonization and claims to the long unoccupied island of Bolama and the adjacent mainland coast. In the late eighteenth century an English naval officer, Philip Beaver, bought Bolama from the local Bijagó king and established a colony which lasted only eighteen months and then was dissolved. The island changed hands several times until the dispute, arbitrated by United States President Ulysses S. Grant in 1870, was resolved in favor of the Portuguese. Border problems with France were worked out in the convention of 1886 whereby Portugal relinquished the port of Zinguinchor on the southern bank of the Casamance for the Cacine district in the south which the French had acquired from the Nalú tribe three decades earlier. In 1879 Portuguese Guiné was separated from the Cape Verde archipelago and established as a separate colony. Bolama was named the capital—a hasty step later to be regretted (Bissau became the capital in 1941).

The newly created colony entered a phase of military occupation and "pacification" which lasted well into the early twentieth century. The warrior tribes remained unsubdued and kept the whites penned within the walls of their cities. Trade was paralyzed, and the budget annually showed a deficit. In 1884 a column of Angolan recruits was cut down, expeditions in the 1890's were unsuccessful, and campaigns in 1901, 1903, 1904, and 1907 only partially subdued the rebellious natives. A Portuguese soldier, Captain Teixeira Pinto, and a Senegalese refugee named Abdul Injai, who served as his lieutenant, set out to complete the conquest of Guiné and accomplish what their predecessors had failed to do. Campaigns against rebellious Africans in 1913 and 1915 were successful. Then Teixeira Pinto went to East Africa, where he was killed fighting Germans. Abdul Injai was rewarded with the chieftainship of Oio, but this despot had to be removed forcibly from his position and exiled to the Cape Verdes as so many of his fellow Africans had been before him. Further campaigns were carried out in 1917, 1925, and 1936, but the Portuguese claim thereafter that the territory had been pacified was offset by ever latent rebellion and resistance among the African tribes. Under New State administration, increased Portuguese restriction of Africans was countered by strikes among urban workers in the 1950's and open warfare by exiled nationalists in the 1960's.

Ethnographic Conflict

Ethnographic differences in Guiné are widespread and must be identified in order to analyze pressures obstructing an African nationalist solution. What little is known of the African in Guiné is contained in the writings of interested Arabs and Europeans in native folklore. The Portuguese writings on the African origins, wars, migrations, kingdoms and institutions, and economic developments not only lack scholarship and depth but contain views partisan to official policy. Despite the dearth of reliable material some details can be sketched.

Portuguese Guiné was once tied to the ancient Sudan empires, the first being that of Ghana beginning in the fourth century. The decline and destruction of the empire of Ghana in the eleventh century was accompanied by the liberation of many subjected tribal groups, among whom were the Mandingas residing partially in Guiné. The influence of Islam resulted in the migration of other tribal groupings, the Beafadas and Nalús in particular, who moved west from Mali to Guiné. By the thirteenth century the Mandinga empire of Mali was established but was in decline by the fifteenth century and had disappeared by the seventeenth. Various animist groupings, including the Fulas a century later, rose to challenge Islamic influence.

With the exception of the later Fula invasion and conquest, and dislocations caused by the Portuguese military and administrative occupation, tribal groupings in the fifteenth century were located more or less as today: first, along the coast and on the adjacent islands, a group of primitive tribes including the Felupe, Baiote, Banhum, Cassanga, Manjaco, Cobiana, Brame, Papel, Balanta, Bijagó, Beafada, and Nalú; second, inland from the coast, the Mandinga kingdoms of Braço and Cabo, partially subject to the Cassanga, Balanta, and Beafada but at the same time strongly influencing and assimilating with those coastal tribes; third, to the south and east there existed the Tiapis, Cocolis, Landumãs; to the interior were the Pajadincas.

Today in Guiné, residing in the low marshy lands along the coast and river estuaries, Africans are dependent upon a subsistence farming economy. Tribal authority structure is based on councils of family chiefs who wield great power. Little influenced by Christianity, these tribes are essentially animist. The Balanta, whose membership exceeds one hundred thousand, is the largest of the coastal tribes, followed in order by the Manjaco, Papel, Brame, Beafada, Bijagó, Felupe, Mansoanca, Baiote, and Nalú. The tall, slender Balanta is industrious and traditionally has been amenable to colonial authority. Along the northwestern coast the Manjaco, resembling the Papel in appearance and customs, is hard-working and a clever trader. The Brames and Felupes, residing on the north bank of the Cacheu, are considered inferior by other tribes. South of the Gêba estuary are the Beafadas, who resemble the Fulas of the interior. The Bijagós predominate on the archipelago of the same name, and the Nalús reside in the southeast coastal corner.

To the interior are the Fula and the Mandinga, respectively the second and third largest tribal groupings. The major Fula tribes are the Fula-Forros in the northeastern interior, the Fula-Pretos further to the west, and the Futa-Fulas to the southeast. In contrast to the Fulas, who are cultivators, the Mandingas are traders and laborers largely scattered throughout Fula territory. The Mandingas subdivide into Saracotés, Bambarãs, Jacancas, Sôssos, and Quissincas. The Fulas and Mandingas differ from the coastal tribes in that they are influenced by Islam. Islamic influence, however, extends only to about 35 per cent of the indigenous population, whereas more than 60 per cent is animist and less than one per cent is Christian.

While serving as an agronomist for the Portuguese government in the early 1950's, Amílcar Cabral attempted to assess the contribution to agricultural production by eighteen of some thirty identifiable tribes in Guiné. Cabral concluded that the tribes cultivated only 12 per cent of the land area and that most land was cultivated by four tribes: Balanta (30 per cent), Fula (nearly 29 per cent), Mandinga (nearly 16 per cent), and Manjaco (nearly 13 per cent). The Mancanha, Papel, Beafada, and Felupe worked a little more than 9 per cent of arable land.

Ethnic differences on the island possessions have already been elaborated. Interestingly, Africans on the Cape Verdes tend to be descendants of the Balanta, Papel, and Bijagó tribes, although most inhabitants are mulatto, symbolizing, as stated by one Portuguese writer, "the undeniable forging of Portuguese culture in the tropics in a way unequaled in the past." Portuguese Guiné was a dependency of Cape Verde until the late nineteenth century. As a result, the *lingua franca* of Guiné remains today the Cape Verde creole influenced by words from the African languages and the Portuguese pronunciation. Furthermore, many high officials and the majority of minor functionaries in Guiné traditionally have been Cape Verdean mulattoes. The small middle class of postal and customs officials, government clerks, and small traders generally have been Cape Verdean.

Economic Stagnation

The economy of Guiné is based almost exclusively on agriculture with most subsistence and export production being in the hands of Africans. Ground nuts, palm kernels, and vegetable oils make up a large share of the territory's export production, whereas rice, maize, cotton, sugar cane, and other secondary products are for domestic consumption. Rubber production for export is small, as is lumber production, although the relatively unexploited forests are being increasingly tapped for the export of hardwoods. Livestock production, principally cattle, sheep, goats, and pigs, is an important part of the indigenous production; exports, however, have declined in recent years. Prospecting for petroleum has yet to yield substantial production. Known deposits of phosphate near Senegal and bauxite near the Guiné border to the south are not yet exploited. Industrialization is insignificant since only a few firms process agricultural products. Lack of electric power and a railway and road system have impeded industrial progress, although the territory is fortunate to possess an elaborate network of canals that intersect its many rivers and estuaries.

In size and population São Tiago is the largest of the Cape Verde islands; its capital, Praia, is also the capital of the archipelago. Only São Tiago and three other islands—Santo Antão, São Nicolau, and Brava—have running streams the year round. São Vicente has no permanent source of fresh water and must import its water from adjacent islands. One island, Santa Luzia, is uninhabited. Lack of rainfall has left the islands little vegetation; soils are poor and suffer from aridity and soil erosion. There is little agricultural production for export (bananas, coffee, and oil seeds) and, in fact, insufficient domestic production necessitates the importation of foodstuffs. There is a small livestock industry, and fish contribute significantly to the domestic food supply. Consequently, the only economic importance of the archipelago is its function as a refueling station for ships and a few aircraft. Also salt, extracted from the islands Sal and Maio, is a principal export.

Once known as the Coco islands, São Tomé and Príncipe today continue to benefit from production of cocoa, the most important cash crop, and also from coconuts and copra, which are mostly exported to foreign countries. Agriculture is thus the principal activity, although most foodstuffs must be imported. There is little industrial development.

For many centuries Guiné, Cape Verde, and São Tomé and Príncipe languished in economic backwardness and stagnation. In the fifteenth and sixteenth centuries the Portuguese sought the spices of the east; although gold was an attraction in the early period, dominance by indigenous elements over the interior minerals prevented its exploitation. Furthermore, mineral and commercial production failed to yield prices as high as slaves. Yet the exploiters of the slave trade diminished local manpower, thereby disrupting the economy. The slave trade brought anxiety and tension to the native masses, and their resistance as well as the challenge of other foreign interests diverted Portugal's attention, principally to the Angolan slave markets. The economy of the mainland and islands suffered from poor organization, lack of taxation, persistent deficits, and general lack of interest by the metropolitan government accompanied by a minimum of administrative personnel.

Under the Salazar regime a protectionist tariff has more or less elminated trade with foreign countries, as was the case prior to the 1930's. Since the early 1950's Portugal has absorbed between 80 and 90 per cent of Guiné's exports and provided about 65 per cent of imports. Likewise, Cape Verde's trade is predominantly with the mother country. São Tomé and Príncipe's cocoa trade with foreign nations makes the islands considerably less dependent on trade with Portugal. A problem related to the trade with Portugal is the monopolization of commerce and finance, respectively, by the large Portuguese Companhia União Fabril (CUF) and the Banco Nacional Ultramarino. Oil and bauxite concessions have been granted to U.S. and Dutch interests but have yet to be exploited fully. In its development plans the Portuguese government has not only favored large private enterprise but has concentrated its attention on improvements in transportation and communications, which has been particularly helpful to the Portuguese military forces' defense against nationalists. Relatively little money has been allocated to the improvement and expansion of agriculture and animal husbandry or to facilitating development of light industry, nor has much been expended on construction of schools and educational facilities, control of endemic diseases, urban sanitation and other public services.

Thus Portuguese Guiné and the island possessions suffer from underdevelopment and stagnation, a fact sometimes recognized by Portuguese officials and African nationalists alike. More than a decade ago Joaquim A. Areal in the official *Boletim Cultural da Guiné Portuguesa* outlined necessary policy changes for the government. Among his suggestions were the provision of technical assistance, farm machinery, and capital to assist the native peasant, raise his income and standard of living, and stimulate overall agricultural production; agricultural planning to utilize effectively all cultivable land; provision of liberalized internal trade with the elimination of oppressive tax and other restrictions; allocation of state and private investment capital to the industrial sector; development of electrical power and such other infrastructure needs as roads, bridges, port facilities, and the like; construction and staffing of technical schools to provide Africans with job training; and the creation of credit facilities for agriculture and industry. Such suggestions, if acceptable to and acted upon by the Portuguese government, might well assure its continued presence in Guiné and the islands. Intransigence and continued neglect of these territories by the government, however, has served to widen the gap of misunderstanding between Portuguese and African, thereby narrowing alternatives and leaving African nationalists with no other choice than to pursue independence and development through violent revolutionary struggle.

African Resistance and Nationalist Ideals

Portuguese difficulties in Guiné and the island possessions are reflected in African resistance to the European presence and exploitation of human and natural resources. In the fifteenth and early sixteenth centuries, Portuguese traders and pioneers experienced difficulty in their commercial and colonization efforts and found themselves subject to taxes and other restrictions imposed by the local African rulers whose sovereignty on the coast of Guiné was absolute. In 1679 the *régulos* (the African chiefs who are subservient to the Portuguese administrator or chief of post and who have attained their position through succession, tribal election, or reward for faithfully having served the Portuguese) of Mata and Mompataz revolted unsuccessfully against the Portuguese at Cacheu on the pretext of having been discriminated against in trade with foreigners. Seventeen years later the Portuguese put down the rebellion of a Christian African, Bibiana Vaz, who desired the profitable trade with French and English merchants. In 1696, Africans seized two Portuguese soldiers and demanded payment and other concessions in return for the hostages. A year later the first of many wars between the Portuguese and the Papéis (plural for Papel) was launched. Led by the *régulo* Incinhate, the Papéis insisted on the liberalization of trade restrictions and an end to the abuses of the slave trade. In the same year the Mandingas attempted to expel the white populace at Farim. Although the Portuguese claimed success in their "pacification" of the Mandingas, thereafter they maintained a military force in Farim to protect the European population.

The wars with the Papéis persisted throughout the eighteenth century. In February 1753 the Papéis, led by the *régulo* Palanca, resisted the Portuguese attempt to rebuild the fort at Bissau. While containing the Africans, the Portugese lost nine men (and the Papéis some five hundred) and for years thereafter were threatened by isolated attacks. In May and June of 1792 the Bijagós attacked the English settlement at Bolama, killing eight and demanding the prevailing price paid for slaves in exchange for the English captives.

Liberalism within Portugal during the early nineteenth century influenced the local European elements in Farim, Cacheu, Gêba, and other townships to establish miniature parliaments which in turn decreed new laws and regulations that antagonized and provoked uprisings in the indigenous population. In May 1824 there was a lengthy battle at Cacheu between Papéis and Portuguese, and not until December of the following year was peace secured. In November 1842 (and in September of 1844 and 1846) there were Papel uprisings in Bissau. In December 1846 *grumetes* allied with Mandingas to attack Farim. Nine years later Gêba was attacked by Africans. In early 1871 the assassination by *grumetes* of the governor of Bissau was followed by a Portuguese military campaign against the *régulos* of Cacanda, Bassarel, Bianga, and Churó. In December 1878 a Portuguese military force was massacred by Felupes near the Bolor river.

The administrative separation of Guiné from Cape Verde in 1879 was followed by intensive military efforts to subdue the rebellious African elements and to occupy effectively the colony of Guiné. Frequently the strategy of the small Portuguese military forces was to encourage intertribal rivalry, thereby undermining the strength of the African resistance to Portuguese occupation. The first move to overcome the African was the establishment in 1879 of a military outpost at Buba where ensued thereafter two decades of military struggle. An attack on Buba in 1880 by Fulas and their *régulo*, Mamadú Paté of Bolola, was followed by further harassment a year later by the *régulo* of Forreá, Bácar Guidalí. A military expedition comprised of one hundred Portuguese soldiers and several hundred Mandingas, Fula-Pretos, and Beafadas subdued Bácar and Mamadú a year later.

'The Portuguese, however, were unable to restrain Bácar, who quickly abrogated the peace treaty and again attacked Buba. Desiring to be *régulo* of Forreá, Mamadú declared war and defeated Bácar, who was assassinated during the struggle. Mamadú became *régulo*, and a treaty of peace was signed with the Portuguese in 1886.

Meanwhile, Portuguese forces defeated the Beafadas at Jabadá in 1882 and a year later launched a campaign against the Balantas. In 1884 a military column was sent to the Cacanda area south of Ziguinchor; Felupes seized a Portuguese gunboat and ambushed a Portuguese patrol. In early 1886 a Portuguese column suffered heavy casualties and retreated at Bijante. In the same year the Portuguese defeated Mussá Moló, who today is revered as a legendary figure in the native folklore of the Senegâmbia region. Mussá and his Fula-Pretos had rebelled against the Fulas, Mandingas, and Beafadas to whom they had been subject for many years. The Fula-Pretos quickly seized control of large areas around Buba and south of the Gambia river. Mussá then harassed the Portuguese at Gêba, attacked river boats and supply trains, and cut communications with Bissau. In July 1886, eighty Portuguese soldiers accompanied by some four thousand Fulas and Mandingas and several hundred Beafadas and *grumetes* attacked Mussá and forced his retreat.

Relative tranquility prevailed in the Gêba region until 1889 when indigenous elements (dissident Fula-Pretos, Mandingas, and Beafadas) again rebelled, thus necessitating the dispatch of a Portuguese military column. A year later a four-month campaign was launched against the warrior Moli Boía, the result being the devastation of many native villages and the flight of Moli to French territory. While the small Portuguese military force attempted to subdue the uprising at Gêba, civil war broke out between Papéis of Antula and Intim, the latter being aided by *grumetes* in Bissau. At the same time Mamadú Paté resumed his attacks on Buba, and Mussá Moló terrorized the region of Farim. Local Portuguese administrators called desperately for reinforcements from nearby Bolama, the Cape Verdes, Angola, and Portugal, and throughout most of 1891 and 1892 Bissau continued in a state of siege. Attempting to contain rebellious natives, a Portuguese column was cut down by Papéis at Intim in April 1891; six officers and 41 soldiers were killed in combat near Bissau a month later. Thereafter, the Portuguese claimed victory over rebellious Africans at Intim, Antula, and Bandim near Bissau, and with the defeat of Mussá the regions around Gêba and Buba appeared to be pacified. However, in December 1893, some three thousand Papéis, assisted by Balantas from nearby Nhacra and Cuntanga, attacked the small fortress of Pijiguiti at Bissau. The following month the Papéis again moved against Bissau, suffered great losses, and by May were overcome by the Portuguese.

The government organized two military operations in 1897, the first against the Manjacos, who were subdued a year later at Caió and the second against Balantas and Mandingas in what is known as the first war of Oio. A Portuguese column overcame several villages before reaching Oio, where an auxiliary force of three thousand Africans commanded by Mamadú Paté and the Beafada régulo of Cuór, Infali Soncó, suddenly defected and turned against the Portuguese troops, inflicting heavy casualties and forcing a hasty retreat.

African hostility continued to preoccupy the government, whose infrequent attempts to pacify Guiné were relatively ineffective. Attention in 1900 was directed to containment of insurgent Bijagós on the island of Canhabaque. A year later military operations were resumed in the region of Oio. In 1904 there was an attempt to put down rebels in the region of Churó near Cacheu. The same year, in an expedition against the Manjacos in the Farim district, government troops were badly defeated with more than four hundred soldiers killed.

That Guiné was seriously threatened by the African insurgents was demonstrated by alarming reports in the metropolitan press that indicated only Bissau remained under effective European control, yet was unable to guarantee the security of its inhabitants. Previously exaggerated reports had been sent to Lisbon about the victories of the government troops. According to a British official who visited Bissau, such reports were "preposterous and absurd," the Portuguese having "failed to conquer the natives whenever they have undertaken military operations against them." The Africans' contempt for the weak, corrupt government increased with the armed expeditions that destroyed hostile villages and killed their inhabitants. Being powerless over the natives, the administration blamed its problem on neglect by Lisbon and resorted to desperate punitive measures against the local peoples. Atrocities were not uncommon.

The former ally but now enemy of the Portuguese, Infali Soncó and his Beafadas began to harass navigation on the Gêba river, successfully impeding commerce between Bissau and Bafatá. At the same time Felupes at Varela along the coast between the Cacheu river and Cape Roxo, Balantas at Góle, and Papéis near Bissau continued to resist Portuguese attempts to collect taxes. Reinforcements were called for and the "Campaign of Guiné" was initiated in 1907 against Infali Soncó. In late November a Portuguese military force disembarked at Xime, subdued the régulos of Badora, Cossé, Bolóli, and Corubal and temporarily liberated much of the region between Xime and Bafatá. Reinforcements from Moçambique and Portugal arrived three months later, and on April 1, 1908, an expeditionary force concentrated at Xime, set out for Bambadinca, crossed the Gêba river, and advanced through the region of Cuór. As the Portuguese advanced upon abandoned native villages, which they plundered and burned, Infali sought refuge in the forested Mandinga territory of Oio; the key Beafada centers of Sambel Nhantá, Gangapatiro, and Ganturé offered little resistance and were occupied, and a military post was established at Sambeliantá.

The second phase of the Guiné campaign focused on the Papel uprising at Bissau. A force of seven hundred Portuguese attacked and destroyed the Papel villages of Intim and Bandim in early May. Several other native villages were destroyed as the expedition moved on Antula returning to Bissau upon receiving word that the Papéis had attacked Bissau itself and burned one of the *grumete* districts. Upon reaching Bissau, the expeditionary force repulsed a Papel night attack. Not until the following year, however, were peace terms with the Papéis agreed upon. In November the Portuguese, in a surprise attack against Balantas near Góle, burned several villages, including Colicunda and Chombe and suffered small casualties while massacring more than one hundred Balantas. In retaliation the Balantas attacked the military post at Góle in February 1909 but after a four-day siege were driven off by Portuguese reinforcements and the support of Abdul Injai, a Fula from French Guinée who had been *régulo* of Cuór in return for services rendered the government.

What the Portuguese commonly call the final phase of pacification began with the arrival of João Teixeira Pinto in 1912. As commander of the Portuguese military force in Guiné, Teixeira Pinto launched four military campaigns. The first, from April until August 1913, centered on the conquest of the Oio region. Teixeira Pinto disguised himself as a trader and personally reconnoitered the previously unknown region. Later, assisted by Abdul Injai and several hundred recruits, Teixeira Pinto reached Mansôa on March 29, where he was attacked by Balantas and Mandingas. Thus began the war of the Oio. After a month of fighting along the banks of the Mansôa river, Teixeira Pinto swiftly moved to the center of the region and occupied Mansoadé and Mansabá, where he established a military post in early June.

Having effectively occupied the Oio, the commander initiated a second campaign which lasted from January to April 1914 and was directed at the Papéis and Manjacos in the Cacheu region, where Teixeira Pinto avenged the deaths of several Portuguese, including the administrator of Cacheu, killed by the Papéis. He and Abdul seized the Papel village of Xurobrique, established a military post, and then moved against the Manjacos by occupying Pelundo and Bula. By April he had advanced to Bassarel and Caió where he constructed two military posts.

The third campaign was against the Balantas of Mansôa during May, June, and July. Teixeira Pinto and Abdul set out for Mansôa to crush the Balantas, who had decimated a small Portuguese force in February and ambushed and killed forty soldiers in March. A month after departing from Bula on May 13, Teixeira Pinto reached Mansôa after overcoming frequent Balanta resistance. Once the military post at Nhacra was built, the region was considered under effective control.

The last of Teixeira Pinto's campaigns took place at Bissau from May to August 1915. In early June, the Papéis attacked Bissau. The Portuguese garrison repulsed the Papéis but suffered 88 casualties. Teixeira Pinto, Abdul Injai, and a force of 1,600 swiftly moved against the Papéis, seized Antula, and swept through Bôr, Safim, Bijimita, and Biombo, where military posts were established. Thus the island of Bissau was secured with a Portuguese loss of 47 killed and more than 200 wounded.

For his services Abdul Injai was appointed *régulo* of Oio. During the campaigns he had murdered, looted, burned villages, killed women and children, and laid waste to considerable areas of the territory. As *régulo* he soon abused his new powers and defied Portuguese authorities. A state of siege prevailed in Bissorã and Farim until Abdul was defeated and captured in August 1919 by a Portuguese expedition. Thereafter he was exiled to Moçambique and the Cape Verdes.

Abdul Injai's disrespect of authority demonstrated that under Portuguese administration Guiné was far from pacified. In March 1917 a state of siege was declared in the Bijagó archipelago and a force was sent to Canhabaque where a military post was created. In July there were military operations against rebellious natives at Nhambalam and a year later in Baiote territory. There were further troubles at Canhabaque in June 1925, and a state of siege was declared on Bissau in September 1931 after a bloody outbreak between Papéis and Mancanhas. Finally, in 1936, the government attempted to end resistance at Canhabaque and sent three columns of regular troops and several hundred auxiliaries to the island. The Bijagós were overcome after a two-month struggle and the government's loss of 35 dead and more than a hundred wounded. Nevertheless, the Bijagós and many other tribes almost everywhere in Guiné passively prolonged their resistance.

After World War II and into the early 1950's, Africans grouped into officially recognized sporting organizations within which protest and dissent persisted. In November 1950 the first and only Guiné labor organization, the Sindicato Nacional dos Empregados do Comércio e da Indústria, was established within the Portuguese corporative structure, but Africans were not allowed to demonstrate or strike. A turning point was reached in 1954 when the government banned the Sports and Recreation Association because its statutes opened membership to both assimilated and indigenous Africans. About the same time several Cape Verdeans permitted to attend schools and universities in Portugal arrived in Guiné. Noteworthy among these Cape Verdeans were Amílcar Cabral and Henri Labery. The former had been educated as an agronomist in Lisbon, where he associated with African students from Angola and Moçambique, through such official organizations as the Casa dos Estudantes do Império and the Centro de Estudos Africanos. Upon graduating with honors from the Instituto Superior de Agronomia in 1950, Cabral served the government in Guiné and Angola before going into voluntary exile. Labery, who had lived much of his life in Guiné but was a Cape Verdean by descent, also attended Lisbon schools and before exiling himself to Senegal visited Portugal several times during the 1950's.

In 1954 (one year after Portuguese police had massacred Africans in São Tomé for protesting labor conditions) Cape Verde and Guiné commercial and civil service employees established the first clandestine nationalist organization, the Movimento para a Independência Nacional da Guiné Portuguesa, which failed and was succeeded in September 1956 by the Partido Africano da Independência da Guiné e Cabo Verde (PAIGC). Headed by Cabral, the PAIGC directed its attention to mobilization of artisans and urban workers, the latter being particularly receptive after port and river transportation workers had successfully struck for better wages in February of the same year. The PAIGC set forth as its fundamental objectives immediate independence of the Cape Verdes and Guiné, the emancipation of the African peoples from colonial exploitation, and the effecting of rapid economic and cultural progress.

Strikes occurred with varying success throughout 1958, but a year later, on August 3, fifty striking dockworkers at Bissau were killed and others wounded in what is referred to by nationalists as the "massacre of Pijiguiti." Twenty-one of those arrested were later tried on charges of subversion and sentenced to prison terms ranging from one to five years. This prompted PAIGC leaders at a clandestine meeting in Bissau during September to revise their strategy. Their eight-point program of action advocated the strengthening of urban organization with the avoidance of public demonstrations and called for the mobilization and organization of the rural peasantry. To carry out this shift of activity from city to countryside, tribal divisions would have to be overcome and nationalist unity achieved. At the same time a clandestine labor union, the União Nacional dos Trabalhadores da Guiné (UNTG), was formed within Guiné. During the subsequent three years of organization, the PAIGC established links with nationalist movements in Angola and Moçambique and joined the Frente Revolucionária Africana para a Independência Nacional das Colónias Portuguesas (FRAIN), formed in Tunis during January 1960 and superseded a year later in Casablanca by the Conferência das Organizações Nacionalistas das Colónias Portuguesas (CONCP).

Several events influenced the PAIGC to assume a more militant role in the nationalist struggle; August 3, 1961, the anniversary of the Pijiguiti massacre, marked the shift from political to direct military action and sabotage. The shift followed a futile appeal in December 1960 (reiterated in October 1961) in which the PAIGC called upon the Portuguese government to commence independence negotiations. In 1960 Amílcar Cabral established in Conakry an exile-based affiliate of the PAIGC called the Movimento de Libertação da Guiné e Cabo Verde (MLGCV), which coalesced exile elements in Conakry and Dakar, including those around Labery. A year earlier, Labery had established in Dakar the Front de Libération de la Guinée Portugaise et du Cap-Vert (FLGC) which brought together representatives of some thirty thousand immigrants from Cape Verde and a few exiles from Portuguese Guiné. At about the same time a rival group, the Movimento de Libertação da Guiné (MLG), was formed by François (Francis) Mendy Kankoila, a Manjaco leader from Guiné who had lived most of his adult life in Senegal. The MLGCV failed, but Cabral, Labery, and other exiled groups formed the Front Uni de Libération de Guinée et du Cap Vert (FUL) in July 1961. Differences over policy prompted another split, and Cabral officially moved PAIGC headquarters to Conakry. Cabral's move was prompted by a series of arrests of suspected PAIGC members, culminating—but not ending—on March 13, 1962, with the arrest in Bissau of Rafael Barbosa, the president of the party's central committee (Barbosa was detained for eighteen months and then released under house arrest).

Immediately following the creation of the FUL, three MLG groups of about 25 men each raided across the border from Casamance, Senegal, their main objective being to attack the administrative post of Suzana and to cut off water and electricity at a small resort hotel in Varela. The Portuguese retaliated by sending troop reinforcements to the border area, by warning Senegal and the Republic of Guinée against any military operation across the border, and by allegedly violating Senegalese airspace in counterattacking the invasion forces, thereby causing Senegal to become the first African country to break relations with Portugal.

Thereafter, the MLG aligned with a Mandinga-oriented nationalist movement in Dakar, called the Rassemblement Démocratique Africain de la Guinée Portugaise (RDAG), into the Frente de Libertação da Guiné (FLG). Subsequently the FLG coalition merged with several other small organizations, including Labery's União das Populações da Guiné (UPG), necessarily renamed because the Cape Verde wing of the old MLGCV had taken an independent course and become the Mouvement de Libération des Iles du Cap Vert (MLICV). The new coalition of the FLG, UPG, and other groups was called the Frente de Luta pela Independência Nacional da Guiné (FLING). The FLING represented several ethnic groups, primarily Fulas, Manjacos, and Mandingas but also Balantas and Papéis. The FLING's inherent tribal divisions kept it a loose coalition constantly undermined by personal disputes and ideological differences. Purges of FLING leaders and groups were not uncommon after 1962. The MLG remained the militant group within the FLING while another, the Union des Resortissants de la Guinée Portugaise (URGP), advocated negotiations with Portugal. The URGP's leader, Benjamin Pinto Bull, visited Lisbon for three days in July 1963 and during the same month his brother Jaime was appointed secretary general of Portuguese Guiné, reportedly the second highest administrative post; these developments raised doubts concerning the seriousness of the group's desire for an independent Guiné.

The extent of the FLING's military action in Portuguese Guiné is difficult to determine. A party communiqué in early 1963 stated that between January and March of the same year FLING militants had been active in sabotage and guerrilla operations in a northern zone (São Domingos and Farim), a central zone (Mansôa, Bissau, and Bambadinca), and a southern zone (Tite, Catió, and Fulacunda) and that the Portuguese had suffered 36 deaths and 117 wounded, while nine FLING soldiers were killed and 36 wounded. Another communiqué, issued in May, claimed that 11 Portuguese soldiers had been killed in the southern zone. A widely publicized attack in northern Guiné that provoked the Portuguese bombing of a Senegalese border town and resulted in condemnation of Portugal by the U.N. Security Council was caused by intertribal rivalry and was not the result of FLING or PAIGC activities. Since 1963 the FLING remained relatively inactive in military operations but reportedly was attempting to organize many of the 37,000 Guiné refugees residing in the Casamance.

In 1962 and thereafter the PAIGC, the main rival to the FLING, established itself as the best organized and most effective of the nationalist movements. With its ranks filled for the most part by Balanta supporters, the PAIGC structured its party pyramid around Cabral, who served as the central committee's secretary for political and external affairs, the party's secretary general, and the liberation army's commander-in-chief. The central committee comprised the secretaries of seven departments (Social and Cultural, Defense and Security, Economy and Finance, Information and Propaganda, Control, Organization and Internal Affairs, Political and External Affairs). The party organization included two national committees (Guiné and Cape Verde), a congress, and a party division into groups or cells, sections, regions, territorial divisions, and zones. After independence, Guiné or Kinara (the name of an ancient kingdom selected by PAIGC leaders as the designation of the new nation) would be organized politically somewhat along the lines of the highly centralized PAIGC structure.

Although it did not concentrate its attention on the Cape Verdes, the PAIGC reportedly was behind a small, abortive uprising in Praia which took place on March 26, 1962. In mid-1962, the PAIGC initiated sabotage within Guiné; its attacks aimed at disrupting communications. Toward the end of the year, PAIGC objectives broadened in an attempt to frustrate and gradually render ineffective the Portuguese armed forces and to establish within the country a nationalist zone of occupation. Full-scale guerrilla warfare continued into 1963 as the PAIGC sporadically attacked Portuguese military barracks and depots, raided and sacked trading posts and towns, destroyed peanut storage bins, and harassed large Portuguese trading companies. The initial PAIGC objective was to profit from the favorable geographical terrain of dense forests and waterways in the south where movement was difficult for the Portuguese but relatively easy for guerrillas whose support was based on the sympathy of the local population. On July 18 the Portuguese Minister of Defense, General Manuel Gomes de Araujo admitted that "well-armed groups . . . have infiltrated our Guiné territory over about fifteen per cent of its surface." Further evidence of nationalist control over much of the area was reported by *The New York Times* correspondent Lloyd Garrison, who in August 1963 visited the town of Catió which he described as "a prison in which the Portuguese have sought shelter . . . No one moves outside the town during the day without a weapon. After dark the barbed wire gates are closed and floodlights illuminate the hostile jungle . . . soldiers based in Catió live in continual tension."

By the end of 1963, PAIGC guerrillas claimed effective control over the greater part of the forested area south of the Gêba river, embracing the inshore island of Como, and as far inland as the points of Buba and Fulacunda. The PAIGC also held pockets of territory to the north of the Gêba near Farim and close to the Senegal border. Furthermore, the PAIGC boasted of defeating 3,000 Portuguese troops who in January 1964 landed on the strategically located island of Como and were forced to withdraw some 75 days later. A PAIGC communiqué reported Portuguese losses "at between 550 and 650 dead and wounded, including the enemy commander." Thereafter, Portuguese operations appeared to continue on a reduced and largely defensive scale as the PAIGC extended its control. During February 13-17, 1964, the party held a conference inside the country and proclaimed that the early phase of guerrilla warfare had passed to a new phase of greater discipline and organization. The country was divided into strategically defined zones of command, a "revolutionary armed forces of the people" was established, and party structure was partially reorganized. Throughout the remainder of 1964, the PAIGC reported successful engagements with Portuguese troops near Novo Lamego, where Fula chiefs traditionally had cooperated with the Portuguese; in the Boé region in the southeast; at Canchungo, where the PAIGC was supported by the local Manjaco population; and at São Domingos and other northern border regions.

Coinciding with the PAIGC political and military activity, Cabral announced in early 1965 that his movement was turning its attention to the economic and social sectors. The PAIGC's economic plan would attempt to raise rice production in liberated zones by twenty per cent, establish interior trade within those zones, create food storage facilities, and destroy the Portuguese monopolies in the territory. Furthermore, an economic survey would be undertaken, and a center for developmental studies of Guiné would be created to deal with the problem of reconstruction in liberated zones. In the social sector a hospital, health centers, and schools would be established and a literacy campaign launched.

By July 1965 the PAIGC claimed control over more than forty per cent of Guiné. Besides gaining complete control over the Boé region, important victories were achieved in Novo Lamego and other regions. On November 4 the PAIGC announced that 732 Portuguese soldiers and nine officers had been killed during rainy season operations from July to October (the

Portuguese acknowledged the death of only 23 soldiers). In January 1966 the government announced the arrests of a "large number" of PAIGC partisans in Farim and the surrounding area, this action taken in retaliation for an earlier nationalist attack on a small village near Farim which according to a Portuguese army communiqué had left the local population "in a state of shock."

That the Portuguese viewed the nationalist challenge in Guiné as a serious matter was revealed in a report published in early 1966 by the official Lisbon newspaper, *Diário de Notícias*. "The enemy whom the Portuguese must destroy is a worthy adversary. Its commanders are well-trained in guerrilla warfare . . . and well-armed. . . . They have shown clear signs of intelligence and a sense of initiative; unless our troops compel them, they never attack forces larger than their own, and they use to the best advantage a difficult terrain which they know like the back of their hands." Indeed the Portuguese were paying dearly—in manpower and in financial resources—for possession of Guiné.

Encouraged by successful native rebellions in Angola and Guiné, African nationalists from Moçambique patched up their differences and in September 1964 launched their independence struggle. To evaluate the significance of this outbreak it is necessary to examine the colonial economic structure and the social and cultural differentiation of ethnic populations in Moçambique. Economic weaknesses and social and cultural differentiations are a result of Moçambique's historical experience, culminating in African native discontent and resistance throughout many centuries of Portuguese rule. Portugal's unwillingness to satisfy Moçambican demands at a time when other African colonies became independent nations led to the emergence of nationalism.

Stretching more than sixteen hundred miles north and south along the east coast of Africa, Moçambique is separated in the north from Tanzania by the Rovuma River and is bounded in the northwest by Lake Niassa (Nyasa or Malawi), Zambia, and Malawi; in the west by Rhodesia; and in the south by South Africa. While varying in width from fifty to seven hundred miles, Moçambique divides roughly into coastal lowlands, which comprise about two-fifths of the total area; an undulating central plateau between five hundred and two thousand feet in height; and a higher plateau and mountainous region to the west and northwest. Intersecting the territory are rivers and fertile valleys within which are concentrated the majority of the nearly seven million inhabitants. Six rivers converge upon Delagoa Bay, while between the capital, Lourenço Marques, and the Zambeze are the Limpopo and Save rivers, which empty into the Moçambique Channel. The Zambeze, the only navigable river, traverses the territory some five hundred miles before pushing through a maze of estuaries to the sea. To the north of the Zambeze are four rivers—the Licungo, Ligonha, Lúrio, and Rovuma.

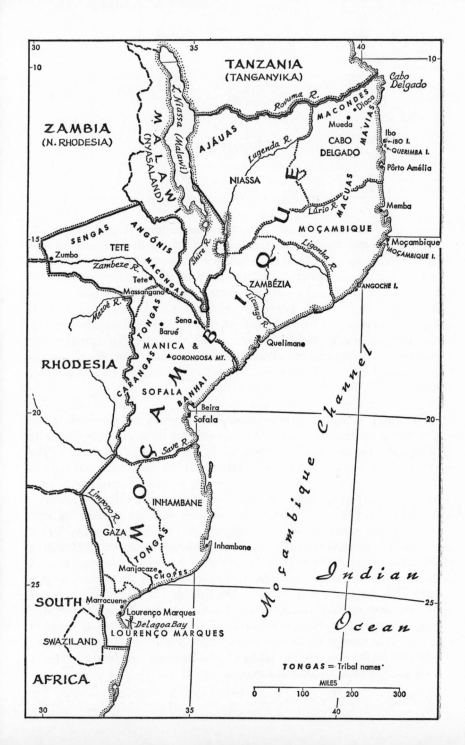

Economic Weaknesses

Moçambique enjoys both a tropical and subtropical climate with a hot, rainy season from November to March and a cool, dry season during the remainder of the year. The territory is primarily agricultural and grows tropical and subtropical crops, which filter through Lourenço Marques and Beira, two of East Africa's busiest ports.

The greatest share of Moçambique's commodity exports derive from six agricultural products: cotton, since 1961 regulated by an autonomous cotton institute; cane sugar, produced for the most part on three large European sugar plantations; cashew nuts, raised principally by African farmers; copra, generally produced on European plantations; tea; and sisal. Other export crops include bananas and citrus, manioc, and timber products. Indigenous subsistence agriculture provides food for most of the African population, although some foodstuffs, wheat grains in particular, frequently must be imported. A potentially important cattle industry is hindered by the tsetse fly, while the fishing industry has yet to be fully organized. The relatively undeveloped mining industry, is limited principally to the production and export of coal and bauxite. Exploration for oil has yielded no deposits, although a refinery operates at Lourenço Marques. Industrialization is at an early stage, despite economic development plans and significant production in cotton textiles and cement as well as in such basic consumer goods as beer, soap, shoes, and the like.

Despite small economic advances and reform legislation in September 1961 that concerned education, increased local autonomy, and accelerated development, the Portuguese in Moçambique face many unresolved economic problems. First, a traditional trade pattern of heavy imports (manufactured goods, machinery, railway and port equipment, and industrial goods) and unfavorable terms for exports result in a perennial trade deficit which is partially offset by invisible exports, namely transit revenues from the coastal ports and the railroads; tourism; and the earnings of migrant workers recruited for work in Rhodesia and South Africa. Another vital problem is the lack of adequate transportation and communication facilities and power which severely hinder economic and industrial development. Furthermore, a lack or shortage of loan funds and investment capital impedes implementation of specific development projects. Other structural weaknesses include a poorly distributed agricultural base; a continued Portuguese monopoly over principal exports; low wage levels for African agricultural workers (per capita income for African males is estimated by the United Nations at about 18¢ daily or $58 annually); and, because of low African purchasing power, a lack of participation in the national economy.

Social and Cultural Differentiation

The population census of 1960 divided Moçambicans into "civilized" and "noncivilized" inhabitants. Only a little more than two per cent (163,000 of the 6.6 million inhabitants) were classified as civilized; of these, some five thousand were Africans, the remainder being Europeans, Orientals, Indians, and mixed. Europeans, who numbered roughly 130,000 in 1966, dominate the political and economic affairs of the territory and occupy the upper level of a highly stratified social system. They control the main administrative positions in government and the important industries and commercial institutions; their Portuguese language and Roman Catholicism officially prevail in national life. Furthermore, the educational system favors the European, whose illiteracy rate is low in contrast to that of the African.

Before the arrival of the Portuguese, Arab influence predominated along the coast where the Macuas (Makuas) adopted Islamic ways; later influence spread inland where Ajáuas (Yaos) imitated the Arabs. Their commercial language was Swahili, the *lingua franca* of East Africa. Along the coast are Monhes or natives who have mixed with Asiatic Muslims.

There are three types of Asians: the Chinese, residing along the coast; the non-Christian Hindus called Banyans, predominantly small traders whose ancestors were introduced into East Africa at the end of the seventeenth century; and the Catholic Goanese traders, shopkeepers, and civil servants, many thousands of whom were expelled from Moçambique after India's absorption of Goa in 1961.

The African is the least privileged of the racial groupings. His ethnic origin is Bantu, a name applied to Negroid peoples who occupy equatorial and southern Africa and who, apart from their languages, do not show great cultural uniformity. Speech and dialects vary from region to region, however. The principal Bantu languages spoken in Moçambique are the Tonga of the southern region; the Nyanja with a variety of dialects spoken along the Zambeze valley; Macua with four distinct dialects in the northeast; and the aforementioned Ajáua. Swahili, the Arabized Bantu speech, is used to some extent in the northeast and along the coast. The religion of the overwhelming majority of Africans is paganistic, ancestral, and traditional worship, although Muslim beliefs are followed by peoples in the north, and Christian missionaries, both Catholic and Protestant, have had some influence elsewhere in the territory.

Tribal divisions are confused by varying interpretations of writers, by the usual tribal use of more than one name, by a variety of affixes by which a tribe is known, and by an amalgamation of many tribes. Another problem is the overlapping of Africans in Moçambique with neighboring peoples in Tanzania, Malawi, Zambia, and South Africa since the nineteenth century colonial powers divided Africa into spheres of influence not coinciding with traditional ethnic distribution. Nevertheless, a classification of native peoples can be sketched, and a synthesis of the writings on ethnic differentiation in Moçambique reveals several Bantu groupings.

The Tongas, believed to have emigrated from West Central Africa during the thirteenth century, dominate the southern region. They are also known as Barongas (from which Tonga was possibly derived) and derogatorily were called the Amatongas by the Ngoni who under the leadership of Soshangane (Manikosi or Manicusse) migrated from the south at the beginning of the nineteenth century, occupied the pasture lands of Gaza, and later predominated in Lourenço Marques, Gaza, and Inhambane districts. These Ngoni, known in Moçambique as the Vatuas or Abagazas, were proud, warlike peoples whose chiefs excelled in administrative affairs and possessed military skills. The Portuguese loosely applied the name Landin to these tribes and to those like the Tongas who came under Ngoni influence. The Tonga grouping resides in two areas, one being south of the Save river and the other to the north in Manica and Barué. In the northern area the Tonga grouping includes widely separated peoples, including the Batonga in the Barué, south of the Zambeze; the Butonga near the border north of the Limpopo; and the Bitonga on the coast near Inhambane, the latter being allies of the Banhai and probably descendants of tribes ruled by the Monomotapa kingdom. Once they were subdued, the Tongas readily adapted to Ngoni organization. They are a pastoral people with a strong taste for European dress and are known for their excellent pottery making; they are traders and are recruited for work in the Transvaal mines of South Africa.

Within and between the two Tonga-occupied areas are remnants of the Caranga (Karanga) tribe which between the thirteenth and fifteenth centuries migrated southward from the eastern side of Lake Tanganyika, settled in the higher country inland, and came under the influence of the paramount chief, the Monomatapa.

Another Bantu grouping, the Chope (Mchope or Ba-shope), resides along the coast north of the mouth of the Limpopo river. Although being a neighbor of the Tonga, the Chope is much less influenced by Ngoni culture; the tribe is known for its musical skills and for the manufacture of special fabrics made from tree bark.

Along the Zambeze, where contact with European civilization has substantially modified many customs and habits, the tribal system is fragmented and dispersed. Ethnographic boundaries are difficult to define, although mention can be made of the Senga (Ba-senga) who occupy a district north of the Zambeze, the Maconga (Makonga), and the Banhai. Also the Angónis (Ba-Angónis) reside in an area along the southwestern shores of Lake Niassa, having earlier migrated from the south to the Save river area where they were conquered by the Vatua and forced to flee northward.

Tribes north of the Zambeze include the Macua grouping in the large area south of the Rovuma river and east of the Lugenda. Known as a sedentary and industrious people, the Macuas are ruled by petty chieftains who wield absolute authority. In the same area are the Mavias and Macondes (Makondes). To the west the Ajáuas inhabit the region between Lake Niassa and the Rovuma and Lugenda rivers. Once an aggressive people but now less so, they dominate the inferior Niassa peoples. They are considered good traders, having historically acted as the intermediaries for tribes of the interior and the Arab traders of the coast. Despite the Islamic influence, they cling to their traditional religious beliefs.

The diversity of tribal traditions, beliefs, and way of life will, of course, be overcome only with the emergence of African nationalism, essentially a nationalism oriented toward development. The Portuguese alternative of Lusotropical integration has had little impact on Moçambique, for social discrimination and cultural determinism are clearly reflected in the guiding philosophy—that Portuguese administration, government, language, Catholicism, and Western European values must prevail. The confrontation between Portuguese and African cultures is severe not only because of Portugal's neglect of the territory, but because few Africans speak Portuguese, the only language allowed in all primary schools. Nor can Africans be expected to develop a political culture premised on Western European values alone, especially when those values represent colonial rule that denies the African effective socialization, political recruitment, and aggregation into Moçambican society. A few years ago anthropologist Marvin Harris succinctly summed up the African's dilemma: "Overwhelmingly illiterate, carefully insulated against provocative news from abroad, subject to corporal punishment and deportation at the whim of the European authorities, their thoughts are never expressed, their real voice unheard . . ."

Early Historical Patterns

The history of Moçambique prior to the voyages of Bartolomeu Dias and Vasco da Gama is somewhat obscured by fragmentary evidence, although many centuries before Christ, Herodotus recorded the circumnavigation of Africa by the Phoenicians, and Arabs of Yemen (known as the people of Sheba) traded regularly in gold and ivory as far south as Sofala. However, three basic patterns of historical development up to the nineteenth century can be briefly examined: they are represented by the Arab, the African, and the Portuguese.

Arab commercial influence, as already noted, had been great long before the arrival of the Portuguese. Arab settlement along the coast probably began in the eighth century. Toward the end of the tenth century the Arabs founded Mogdishu and Brava along the Benadir Coast. Thereafter, Persians established Kilwa, and Kilwa and Mogdishu became powerful states with the latter controlling Sofala which quickly became a center for gold and iron production and the chief source of prosperity to the Arab settlements during medieval times. Eventually Kilwa captured Sofala and became the principal coastal power whose domination included Malindi, Mombasa, Zanzibar, Moçambique island, and trading ports on the islands of Comoro and Madagascar. There was no attempt, however, to occupy the interior. By the end of the fifteenth century and about the time of the Portuguese arrival, Kilwa was in decline and its position was challenged by several independent states and in particular by its chief rival, Mombasa.

After the establishment of Portuguese control at points along the east coast of Africa, Arab influence remained latently strong but was severely limited by Portuguese trade restrictions and the monopolization of gold commerce which resulted in Arab impoverishment and near extinction along the coast. The Portuguese grip on the coastal trade was challenged by the Arabs during the seventeenth century, first by the capture in 1622 of Ormuz and subsequent uprisings at Mombasa, Zanzibar, and other strategic coastal points. A Portuguese settlement at Zanzibar was destroyed in 1652, Moçambique was attacked in 1669, and with the complete loss of Mombasa early in the eighteenth century, Portuguese sovereignty was destroyed north of Cabo Delgado. The loss of Mombasa, according to historian Eric Axelson, "demonstrated that it was manifestly futile to attempt to convert the Muslims of the Swahili coast to Christianity; they were unassailable."

The African dominated the interior of Moçambique and other parts of East Africa both before and after the Portuguese arrival at the end of the fifteenth century. According to early Arab writings, the Zanj tribe moved southward to the Zambeze and inhabited the country as far as Sofala while beyond Sofala the Waq-wags, believed to be Bushmen, dominated. The Zanj, who also occupied Malindi and other coastal centers, were fishermen and hunters but also produced iron and engaged in commerce. The first Bantu wave into Moçambique was probably by Tongas who in about the thirteenth century moved down the Zambeze valley to the coast and gradually extended southward. From Tanganyika came the Caranga tribe which settled inland in higher country. During the latter half of the sixteenth century the Mazimba, a warring, cannibalistic tribe invaded Moçambique from the west, raided Portuguese settlements along the Zambeze until a peace was established in 1592. The last invasion by Africans into Moçambique seems to have been the Ngoni migrations from the south into the Gaza region.

In contrast to the Arab, whose trade with the African was successful, the Portuguese encountered hostility and resistance in the interior. A persistent challenge to the ambitions of the Portuguese was the Monomotapa or paramount chief whose supremacy rested on the possession of the gold mines of Manica and on the gold trade with the Arabs at Sofala. This relationship of many centuries was altered by the Portuguese construction of a fortress at Sofala and the suppression of the Arab trade. Portuguese sovereignty, however, was restricted only to a small area circling the fortress, but it was through Sofala that commercial ties were maintained with the interior African kingdoms.

The hostility of the Monomotapa to the Portuguese was particularly evident throughout the seventeenth century. At the beginning of the century the Monomotapa, named Gatsi Rusere, found himself challenged by rival chiefs and called upon the Portuguese for military assistance which was provided. After several struggles, Gatsi Rusere succeeded in putting down his rebellious rivals and in gratitude for Portuguese support, he promised to relinquish his silver mines on the condition that Portugal help him to consolidate and conserve power. Having defeated his chief rival, Matuzianhe, but failing to receive any tribute from the Portuguese who roamed his lands, the Monomotapa began to raid their camps, thereby not only denying them the silver mines but also disrupting the gold trade.

About 1613 a Portuguese expedition barely defeated a rebellious chief, Chombe, of the Sena region in the Zambeze valley. For the first time in the region, a native force fought Europeans with firearms. Only after several months of fighting did the Portuguese defeat the native chief and prevent the lower Zambeze from being closed to the munitions, trade goods, and reinforcements that customarily were supplied to Tete and nearby Portuguese centers.

Meanwhile, the Portuguese and the Monomotapa continued to engage in small skirmishes. In 1652 the Monomotapa, Mavura, died and Dominican friars invited a son, who was sympathetic to the Church, to become the Monomotapa. The new chief was baptized with the name Dom Domingos. He died a few years thereafter and the Monomotapa's successors again reasserted their independence and reverted to their pagan ways.

Toward the end of the century a minor chieftain and subordinate to the Monomotapa, Changamire, established himself as ruler of the Batua kingdom to the west and then routed the Monomotapa's army and turned against the puppet chief's Portuguese supporters. In 1693, Changamire attacked the Portuguese settlements of the interior, destroying the important settlement of Dambarare. Two years later he attacked Manica but died soon after, just as most of the interior had fallen within his domain. Despite Changamire's death, his success against the Portuguese and their puppet, the Monomotapa, ended Portuguese political influence beyond the present borders of Moçambique. With his defeat the Monomotapa lost all influence in the interior during the eighteenth century; he and his descendants retained only a small area south of the Zambeze.

The third early historical pattern was set by the Portuguese whose imperial design in East Africa involved a confrontation with the Arab and the African. Portuguese objectives were twofold: to substitute their economic and religious influence for that of the Arabs and to ensure control over the East African coast, the gateway to the riches of the Far East.

The Portuguese seized Kilwa where they erected a fortress; they captured and destroyed Mombasa and Sofala and built fortresses; and they secured Moçambique island which by the mid-sixteenth century was the chief Portuguese center along the East African coast. As a result, the East African trade became a royal monopoly with all trade filtering through that insular commercial center while Arab trade diminished where Portuguese authority reigned supreme. At the same time Portuguese East Africa was incorporated into the Portuguese State of India and therefore became dependent both administratively and economically on that Far East possession.

The imperial design shifted from King Manuel's early sixteenth century policy of maritime supremacy to King Sebastião's ambitions to found an African empire, a desire that led to the disastrous crusade in Morocco. The

Portuguese recognized that their interest and control of the east coast of Africa was dependent not only on the commercial and military chain of centers along the coast but also on relations with the African tribes which dominated the hinterland between the Zambeze and the Limpopo. Whereas most Portuguese dealings with the African were confined to the trading centers at Querimba, Ibo, Inhambane, and Delagoa Bay in present-day Moçambique, several attempts were made to penetrate the interior during the sixteenth century. Early attempts to establish permanent stations on the Zambeze in 1513, at Sena in 1531, and at Tete proved unsuccessful, but later an agreement with the Monomotapa banned Mohammedans from his territory and allowed Christian missionaries. The agreement gave the Portuguese control over the gold trade, assuring Sena as a distribution center for trade from the coast and Tete as the center for trade with the Monomotapa.

During the seventeenth century the Portuguese turned to the task of conquering the Monomotapa and exploiting his gold mines. Early in the century the Monomotapa ceded his mines to the Portuguese on the condition that they help him to retain power. This being accomplished, the Portuguese attempted to occupy the area, only to encounter a hostile Monomotapa. In 1628 the Portuguese defeated the Monomotapa Capranzine and about a year later named his successor, Mavura Mhande, who agreed to Portuguese conditions by becoming a Christian and ceding the gold mines. Mavura's successor also became a Christian, and thereafter until the 1690's the hinterland was a prosperous dominion for the Portuguese. The establishment of the *prazo* system by the Portuguese resulted in the replacing of the native chiefs with a class of large estate owners who wielded absolute power and authority over their native subjects and who tended to operate independently of royal control. A subsequent decline of Portuguese influence at the end of the seventeenth and during the eighteenth centuries was accompanied by the substitution of the slave for gold as the chief commercial commodity.

Axelson cites many reasons for the rapid decline of Portuguese influence in East Africa at the close of the seventeenth century. First, a shortage of manpower, a lack of shipping and other resources coupled with the competition of European powers, and the tenuous tie of East Africa with Goa greatly weakened Portugal's position. Second, Portugal failed to resolve the problems of government, and the colony was ruled generally by corrupt and inefficient administrators. Furthermore, the monopolization of the gold and ivory trade considerably reduced the economic influence of the Arabs along the coast. Instead of allowing the Arabs a percentage of the profits of the trade, Axelson concludes that "in trying to get too much, Portugal lost nearly everything."

Pacification and Discontent

Two major rebellions damaged Portuguese prestige in East Africa during the nineteenth century. The first was initiated by a half-caste, Joaquim José da Cruz or Nyaude, who established his headquarters at Massangano and levied tolls on all traffic along the Zambeze. Portuguese attacks against Cruz failed in 1853 when Cruz's son, António Vicente or Bonga, destroyed the town of Tete and again in 1869 when a Portuguese expedition against Massangano was routed, leaving Bonga in control of a large expanse of the territory until his death in 1885. His brother carried on the Cruz tradition until the Portuguese succeeded in capturing Massangano three years later and in deporting the rebels from East Africa.

The second blow to Portuguese prestige was the invasion into the Gaza region by several Ngoni tribes which, fearing the tyranny of the African ruler Chaka, fled in all directions over southeastern Africa. Those who came to Portuguese territory were led by Soshangane, who swept across the lands of the Tonga, crossed the Limpopo, and settled on the grazing lands beyond where they became known variously as Gazas, Vatuas, Shanganas, or Landins. They eventually came into conflict with the Portuguese. At Lourenço Marques they besieged the Portuguese fortress and massacred its garrison. They attacked Inhambane in 1834 and Sofala in 1836; overran the *prazos* south of the Zambeze and occupied Sena; pushed the Angóni to their present area near Lake Niassa; and raided the interior of Mashonaland, effectively overcoming the tribes formerly subject to Changamire.

Soshangane died in 1859, leaving two sons to struggle for control of the vast kingdom that stretched from the Zambeze to south of the Limpopo. By agreeing to cede some of the kingdom in exchange for Portuguese support, Umzila or Muzila defeated the legitimate successor, Mahueva, who, like his father, opposed the Portuguese. Thereafter recognized as chief of Gaza, Umzila maintained official relations with the Portuguese although he continued to raid their settlements and landholdings and to demand tribute. He died in August 1884 and was succeeded by a son, Gungunhana (Gungunyana or Medongazi), whose pragmatism allowed him, on the one hand, to cooperate with the increasingly active Portuguese and, on the other, to look to the British as a potential ally.

The Bonga rebellion and the African challenge left Portugal in a weakened and precarious position. Early in the century the Gaza invasions resulted in the abandonment of the *prazos* and in the owners' selling the inhabitants of their *prazos* as slaves. Consequently, agricultural production declined and effective occupation of the interior altogether ceased. At the same time the British staked out claims on Portuguese territory. In 1823 Captain W. F. Owen had arranged several treaties with native chiefs in the Delagoa Bay region. These treaties became the basis for British claims to a portion of the bay and neighboring lands. Although the dispute was arbitrated in Portugal's favor in 1875 and treaties in 1886 with Germany and France recognized Portugal's claims to the territory between Moçambique and Angola, the British issued an ultimatum in January 1890. The National Assembly at first rejected a proposed settlement, but there was a realization that the British South Africa Company, under Cecil Rhodes, might push its frontiers to include the Manica plateau, Beira, and the Gaza district. A *modus vivendi* was reached, and a final agreement in 1891 limited Portugal to control over the territory comprising Moçambique today.

The treaty represented an end to Portugal's desire to link its west and east African possessions. Internal African disorders also threatened the colony. In the Gaza region Gungunhana apparently consented to British protection over his dominions in return for ceding both Beira and the mouth of the Limpopo to the British South Africa Company. He sent two envoys to London and although hesitant to join native insurgents, he encouraged them to move against Lourenço Marques in October 1894, prompting retaliatory action by the Portuguese. Not until the arrival of reinforcements and the colonial administrator, António Ennes, were the Portuguese able to subdue the insurgents, whom they defeated at Marracuene in early February 1895. Negotiations having failed, the Portuguese force moved against Gungunhana. The Africans suffered losses of more than three hundred in a battle on September 8 and a similar number on November 7. The Gaza force was defeated, its capital Manjacaze seized, and Gungunhana captured on December 28. Gaza became a military district under Portuguese control. Further native agitation recurred, however, and not until the death of Maguiguana, Gungunhana's great military leader, in August 1897 was Gaza declared "pacified."

The interior of the colony remained relatively unoccupied, and to alleviate that situation the government encouraged the formation of chartered companies. The resources of these companies, however, were not great enough to assure occupation of the territories assigned to them nor to ensure Portuguese sovereignty over the colony. Foreign enterprise and capital controlled the port of Beira and a few mining enterprises; the *prazos* of the interior, particularly in Zambézia and in Barué, were in revolt; and Niassa and Moçambique districts were independent of Portuguese administration. It was decisive action and the launching of a series of military campaigns that within a generation would assure Portuguese occupation of the regions of Manica, Zambézia, Moçambique, and Niassa. At the signing of the 1891 treaty with Great Britain, Manica was in a state of revolt. Military expeditions launched against insurgents in Barué were defeated, allowing that region a decade of complete independence while African influence extended to the southern bank of the Zambeze and to the Tonga *prazos*. In 1902 a Portuguese force of three hundred moved against Barué, defeated the rebellious African chiefs in the region, and established a fortress to maintain military control. In 1915, however, sporadic outbreaks took place in Barué, Gorongosa, Sena, Manica, and Zumbo. Not for two years was a Portuguese military force able to suppress the revolt.

In the vast, fertile region of Zambézia, Africans had been granted *prazo* holdings, the objective being to extend Portuguese influence throughout Zambézia and beyond. Important among these *prazo* holders was the Lobo clan, which controlled the Zumbo district and 16 of the 34 *prazos* leased by the government. There were attempts to break the power of these *prazo* owners who refused to pay taxes and obey government directives and whose raiding brought the Portuguese into disrepute. Unsuccessful expeditions were sent to the region in 1869, 1887, and 1888, and the Portuguese suffered two military defeats in 1891. In 1895 the Zambézia Company divided the *prazo* holdings north of Tete, an area ruled by the descendants of the Pereira clan whose defiance of government authority was not really overcome until the arrival of a government expedition in 1902. In September and October 1898 a Portuguese victory was achieved in the war of Maganja. The district of Angonia, along the Nyasaland border, was occupied by the company in 1899-1902. The Lobos joined with other *prazo* owners and with natives and continued to resist Portuguese control. An expedition in 1904 finally secured the region and also suppressed a revolt of Chioko natives west of the Mazoé river.

Before 1890, Portuguese occupation and influence in the Moçambique district had been limited to the island of Moçambique while the coast remained in the hands of the powerful Mohammedan chiefs of mixed Arab and Macua blood whose external relations were dependent on trade with Zanzibar. Early Portuguese attempts to subdue the mainland had ended in disaster. Under the governorship of Mousinho de Albuquerque a serious effort began to occupy the district. On the mainland opposite Moçambique, Mousinho waged a campaign against the Namarrães in 1896-1897. It was only partially successful and allowed him to establish a few military posts along the coast. Even the coast was poorly secured, however, as the Namarrães in 1898 overran one Portuguese post, forcing the dispatch of troops. In 1903-1904, military operations were directed at occupation of Angoche, but only in 1906 was an attempt made to occupy all of the Moçambique district. Marave, the most important of the rebellious Namarrães chiefs, was defeated and other coastal chiefs overcome. Operations continued in Angoche and by 1910 the sultan of Angoche and Farelay was deposed. During 1912 and 1913 military columns moved against Memba and there were further encounters with the Namarrães. Four expeditions were sent to the Moçambique district during 1914-1918.

At the time of the establishment of the Nyassa (old spelling for Niassa) Company in 1893, Portuguese occupation was limited to the island of Ibo and a few coastal military posts to the north. The interior was dominated by the Macua and Ajáua chiefs. Although in 1899 a Portuguese expeditionary force attacked Mataca, an Ajáua and the most important of the chiefs, the area remained unsubdued for many years. The Mataca died in 1903, but his successor denied Portugal the opportunity of asserting its authority until the effective occupation of the territory was carried out in 1908-1912. During 1909 and 1910 the Portuguese moved against the Macua and Maconde tribes, and in the autumn of 1912 a major expedition was directed at the prestigious Ajáuas. The Mataca fled to the neighboring German-occupied territory of Tanganyika, his tribe was subdued, and a string of posts was established to ensure continued Portuguese occupation.

Nationalism and the Independence Struggle

Nationalism in Moçambique is rooted in the pattern of continued resistance that characterized the African population during the first half of the twentieth century. This resistance, as recorded by African nationalists, was evidenced by occasional protests of African dockworkers in Lourenço Marques during the late 1930's; a popular uprising in 1948 at Lourenço Marques, resulting in the deportation to São Tomé and imprisonment of several hundred Africans; another revolt in the district of Inhambane caused by the poisoning of foodstuffs destined for the African population because of a bad harvest; and a 1956 protest in Lourenço Marques that resulted in the death of 49 dockworkers. African nationalist leaders cite further incidents in their ephemeral writings. In April 1960, for example,

Kibiriti Diwani and other members of the Maconde tribe, who had been denied a petition to establish an African association, were arrested in Mueda and deported to an unknown destination but not before police reportedly killed more than six hundred Africans, including several prominent chiefs who had protested the detention of their leaders. In May 1961, police killed Zimbambira Chicusse, a paramount chief of Angonia, and five other chiefs who had been arrested and detained since 1955 for organizing a protest. During the same month police fired upon and killed fifteen laborers from Milange who were seeking pay increases. In August 1963, Lourenço Marques dockworkers demonstrated over the failure of authorities to pay a promised wage increase. In December 1964 and in May 1965 police arrested several prominent African intellectuals, including Rui Nogar, a poet, and Malagatana Goenha Valente, an artist and poet. Some two thousand arrests were made by Portuguese police in the twelve-month period following the outbreak of nationalist guerrilla warfare in September 1964.

Nationalism also evolved within several African associations. *O Brado Africano* was established early in the 1920's as one of the first African weeklies on the continent. Although controlled by the Salazar government, it remains African-oriented. The Grêmio Africano, established for the "civilized" mulattoes or mixed Africans, later became known as the Associação Africana. The Instituto Negrófilo, represented by black Africans and later renamed the Centro Associativo dos Negros de Moçambique, was banned in 1965 for alleged subversion and terrorism. The Associação dos Naturais de Moçambique, was founded, supported, and controlled by whites born in Moçambique. Although at first it openly discriminated in membership and services, in the 1950's the Associação began to encourage membership by Africans and eventually adopted a policy supporting social integration between whites and Negroes and favoring independence. The government intervened, however, and replaced the Associação's leadership, thereby ending its effectiveness and, according to nationalist leader Eduardo Mondlane, "with its demise as a multiracial nucleus may have gone all the hopes for a racially tolerant Moçambique."

Outside Moçambique, nationalists organized several movements whose principal objective was immediate independence for the territory, either through negotiation with the Portuguese or militant struggle. The União Democrática Nacional de Moçambique (UDENAMO) was first established in Rhodesia by exiled nationalists working in Salisbury. Founded on October 2, 1960, it transferred headquarters to Dar es Salaam in April 1961. A second nationalist organization, the Moçambique African National

Union (MANU), was an amalgamation of several small groups, including the Moçambique Maconde Union of northern Moçambique and Tanganyika. Founded in Mombasa, Kenya, during February 1961, MANU was supported by the Kenya African National Union (KANU) and the Tanganyika African National Union (TANU). After Tanganyika was granted independence, MANU moved its headquarters to Dar es Salaam. A third organization, the União Africana de Moçambique Independente (UNAMI), was established in Malawi by exiled leaders from the Tete region. In 1961 it also moved its headquarters to Dar es Salaam.

In June 1962 UDENAMO, MANU, and UNAMI formed the Frente de Libertação de Moçambique (FRELIMO) under the leadership of Eduardo Mondlane, a former university professor whose obtaining of a primary school certificate in 1936 was at the time "the highest educational achievement allowed an African in Moçambique." Mondlane found his way to Portugal and to the United States, earned his doctorate at Northwestern University, and worked with the United Nations as a research officer until 1961 when he joined the faculty at Syracuse University. With the nationalist unification, however, Mondlane returned to Dar es Salaam.

A party congress was held in September to outline a program. The congress condemned Portuguese colonialism and political, economic, and social oppression as well as Portugal's unwillingness to recognize Moçambique's independence. A series of resolutions called for unity among Moçambicans; promotion of literacy programs; establishment of schools and trade unions; instruction in self-defense for the people; cooperation with nationalist groups in Angola, Portuguese Guiné, and the Cape Verde islands; and the seeking of diplomatic, moral, and material help for the freedom struggle in Moçambique.

Mondlane defined Moçambique nationalism as "characterized by the development of attitudes, activities, and more or less structured programs aimed at the mobilization of forces for the attainment of self-government and independence." Mondlane argued that through the political and military programs of FRELIMO national consciousness among individuals and groups as well as the specific goals of self-government and independence could be attained.

With this political philosophy as the basis for his FRELIMO, Mondlane began the difficult task of organization and preparation for the ensuing militant struggle. From its inception, however, FRELIMO was plagued by internal dissension. Well before the front's establishment, one of the leaders and founders of UDENAMO, Hlomulo Chitofo Gwambe, had announced UDENAMO's intention of liberating Moçambique by revolutionary and military means. Since Gwambe was believed to be an agent paid by the Portuguese, he was asked to leave by the government of newly independent Tanganyika. Later he was not named a member of FRELIMO's central committee. Thus ostracized, Gwambe formed the Comité Secreto da Restauração da UDENAMO in Kampala, Uganda, and later officially re-established UDENAMO, this time with a modified name, the União Democrática Nacional de Monomotapa (UDENAMO-Monomotapa).

A second schism occurred after Mondlane returned to his teaching duties at Syracuse University. In mid-1962 and in December several FRELIMO members and many of the former leaders of UDENAMO, MANU, and UNAMI were expelled. Thus Paulo José Gumane and David J. M. Mbunda, secretary general and deputy secretary general respectively of FRELIMO, in 1962 established in Cairo a new UDENAMO, the União Democrática Nacional de Moçambique (UDENAMO-Moçambique). Likewise, Mathew Mmole, treasurer of FRELIMO until his expulsion, reorganized the MANU.

On May 20, 1963, the Frente Unida Anti-Imperialista Popular Africana de Moçambique (FUNIPAMO) was constituted in Kampala under the leadership of Mmole, Gwambe, and Sebastene Sikauke, the provisional representative of the Moçambique African National Congress (MANCO). With the expulsion of six members of the FRELIMO central committee a year later, the Moçambique Revolutionary Council (MORECO) was created. In early 1965, MORECO joined UDENAMO and in mid-June 1965 the Comité Revolucionário de Moçambique (COREMO) officially proclaimed itself a coalition of five movements: UDENAMO-Monomotapa, UDENAMO-Moçambique, MANU, MANCO, and UNAMI.

Despite internal dissension FRELIMO continued its organizational efforts. While financial support was sought for Moçambicans to study in Europe and the United States, the Instituto Moçambicano was founded in Dar es Salaam by Mondlane's American-born wife, Janet; its purpose was to provide educational facilities in training for some of the many thousands of Moçambique refugees in Tanganyika. Meanwhile, FRELIMO soldiers were sent to Algeria and the United Arab Republic to receive military training. Finally, on September 25, 1964, FRELIMO announced that its guerrilla war had been launched within Moçambique.

FRELIMO's initial attacks were directed simultaneously at ten military posts along Lake Niassa and in the Zambézia region. Later FRELIMO reported that between September 25 and October 3 twenty Portuguese soldiers had been killed during sporadic attacks throughout northern Moçambique. The nationalists admitted three deaths while the Portuguese denied reports of trouble within the territory although they claimed the capture of "five groups of terrorists of various nationalities" that attempted to enter Moçambique from Tanganyika. Meanwhile thousands of panicked refugees swarmed across the Rovuma River into Tanganyika, an exodus caused principally by military activity around Mueda, where all houses reportedly were set afire by Portuguese soldiers. The Portuguese also continued building airstrips along the border at Mueda and other points.

By early 1965, a Portuguese communiqué acknowledging the death of only three soldiers since the revolutionary outbreak was countered by the FRELIMO claim that 365 soldiers had been killed in skirmishes in the districts of Niassa, Cabo Delgado, and Zambézia and that 83 Portuguese soldiers were killed in a surprise attack at Diaca on New Year's Day. Nationalist claims during January-July 1965, including New Year's Day, totaled another 525 Portuguese killed in action. By November FRELIMO announced that its 2,000 troops had occupied "large areas" of Moçambique, including complete control of the Cabo Delgado district. The extent of FRELIMO control over a battle zone adjacent to Lake Niassa and stretching twenty to forty miles inland from Tanzania to the Malawi border was confirmed by a series of reports published in the Rhodesian press. After ten days in the area, reporter Lord Kilbracken stated that "in three thousand terrorized square miles the Portuguese, both civil and military, are confined to five small garrisons . . . Not one white settler dares stay in the area . . . The FRELIMO are a tough and elusive enemy . . . at home in the jungle and bush, where they live off the country, striking silently by night, withdrawing swiftly into the dense cover if the Portuguese reply in strength."

SEVEN

PROSPECT AND RETROSPECT

This book focuses on historical trends and patterns. Attention is directed to both the Portuguese and African roles in influencing developments since the fifteenth century, although particular emphasis is given to contemporary activities. In summation, then, let us synthesize these trends and patterns into several propositions and suggest some alternatives for the future of Portuguese Africa.

A Set of Propositions

The initial success of Prince Henry and other heroes of the early period of discovery and expansion was a basis for the mystique and policy that permeated Portuguese thought. That policy was premised on commercial expansion and control of markets—gold, ivory, and slaves in Africa and spices in Asia—through the establishment and maintenance of a string of strategically located garrisons scattered about the world. To some extent also the martyred King Sebastião bolstered the Portuguese imperial dream, for among the young king's objectives was the creation of a vast domain stretching across southern Africa. Not only was that territorial objective not achieved, but the gap between the Portuguese imperial dream and reality was widened by the absence of a comprehensive scheme of administration and settlement. Commercial relations with the African natives and Arab traders deteriorated as the Portuguese centralized control of markets. Lacking financial and human resources, economic development lagged until the empire became a substantial liability and a drain on the reserves of the mother country.

A second proposition, derived from the first, involves the pattern of barter or purchase of one commodity for another, this being the basis for Portuguese imperialism which brought wealth to the metropole, especially during the early sixteenth century. Through systematic establishment of fortresses along a littoral, the Portuguese exploited commercial markets. Imperial exploitation was limited to domination over the exchange of commodities along the coast (principally ivory and gold) for the spice trade of Asia, and little serious effort was made at conquering the extensive hinterland and extracting its natural resources. The spice trade and the Asian empire collapsed, however, and the rationale for the Portuguese presence in eastern Africa disappeared. Neither gold nor other precious metals was found in substantial quantities in Africa, and therefore Portuguese imperialism became almost exclusively linked to a slave economy. The west coast of Africa, the labor reservoir for the Brazilian sugar plantations, grew in importance until the slave trade was suppressed, resulting in the neglect and decline of Angola in particular.

In the late nineteenth century European attention focused on the conquest and division of Africa. The thrust of imperialism demanded large quantities of raw materials from Africa. In return the industrializing European nations exported manufactured goods to Africa. Beset with political and economic difficulties at home, Portugal followed the pattern of other colonial powers and established the chartered company as the instrument of the new imperialism, although this experiment differed from that of other nations in that the capital of the Portuguese African chartered companies was principally foreign.

A third proposition suggests that the patterns of Portuguese imperialism and colonialism were determined in large part by traditional structural weaknesses in the metropole itself. Portugal has been and still is an underdeveloped country. Enveloped in dictatorial order, Portugal depends upon the police and the armed forces as well as an oligarchy of landowners and industrialists who control the economy through a network of cartels and a series of interlocking directorships that link finance and industry. At the same time foreign capital, tied to the oligarchy, has extensively penetrated the economy. The oligarchy stands apart from the masses in a highly stratified society that has yet to implement the extensive welfare programs of some other European countries. Cultural life has been long suppressed and backward. These tendencies of the metropolitan complex determine the direction of overseas domination which the English writer Perry Anderson classifies as "ultra colonialism—that is, at once the most *primitive* and the most *extreme* modality of colonialism."

Fourth, the Portuguese colonies in Africa cannot be viewed as "modern" in outlook. As stated earlier, progress, reform, social change, and structural development are not usually manifestations of imperialism, colonialism, and dictatorship. Portuguese Africa is no exception to this rule. The politics of Portuguese Africa is dominated and controlled by a rigid colonial administrative complex. In the overseas territories economic development has been impeded by a lack of capital, inadequate transportation facilities, and a scarcity of skilled industrial workers; although recent foreign investment, encouraged by mining concessions and other incentives, allows for exploitation of some raw materials and at the same time assists Portugal in maintaining its control over the territories—a development reminiscent of foreign capital participation in the chartered companies established at the end of the last century. Traditionally, social conditions in Africa have reflected the lack of concern for health, unemployment, and education in the metropole. Not unlike black peoples elsewhere, few natives in the Portuguese territories have been permitted to meet the rigid educational requirements, and the educational system itself serves no more than a small percentage of the African population. Likewise cultural progress has been insignificant, although there has been an attempt to cultivate a colonial literature.

Fifth, the African response to Portuguese imperialism and colonialism was deeply rooted in a persistent pattern of resistance, sporadically manifested in the early periods of Portuguese domination and more clearly evidenced in the nineteenth and twentieth centuries when the Portuguese attempted to subdue by military force the African population and to achieve the effective occupation of the African possessions. Thus Moçambique was presumably pacified, the process initiating with the reduction of the Gaza region in the 1890's and terminating with the occupation of the Moçambique district in 1918. In Angola, military expeditions systematically conquered the territory by overcoming the interior resistance and establishing military posts to maintain order over native tribes. Only after many years of struggle was Angola brought fully under Portuguese control toward the end of World War I. In Guiné the task of overcoming the rebellious African was finally completed in 1936.

African resistance did not cease in 1936, however. Sporadic outbreaks of discontent can be documented in the African territories throughout the 1940's and 1950's. A sixth proposition therefore may be premised on this continuous pattern of sporadic resistance that eventually evolved into organized rebellion as the small educated African elite, long frustrated by its subservient role in colonial society, chose first to pressure the intransigent rulers for moderate changes in policy and later to demand independence and nationhood. Spurred on by the wave of emerging independent nations elsewhere in Africa, the African leaders began the arduous task of organization and politicalization that accompanies successful nationalist attempts to challenge colonial authority and rule.

The evolution of nationalism from the Portuguese variant of mysticism kindled by nostalgic memories of the discoveries and expansion to the emergence of African sentiments about nationhood constitutes a seventh proposition. Portuguese nationalism is the basis for a tie between colonies and motherland, for Portugal, according to official accounts, liberated the African continent from Arab domination. The multiracial origin of the Portuguese gave them a special capacity to live in all kinds of climates and conditions and to assimilate all peoples of all races into "one nation" of provinces scattered about the world. Everywhere, according to the official view and that of Gilberto Freyre, the Portuguese brought indigenous peoples into contact with civilization. The Portuguese must preserve this historical heritage and maintain continuity and solidarity with past, present, and future. Survival of order in Africa is dependent on moral unity, which is strengthened by trust for hierarchical authority and confidence in the unbreakable alliance of all Portuguese in the Lusitanian community.

Within this context of Portuguese nationalism, there emerged in the late 1940's and early 1950's a privileged elite of educated African intellectuals which at first tolerated Portuguese colonial policy and found itself unable to defend the interests of the African community. Quickly disenchanted by Portugal's favoring a civilized elite over the African "natives" and searching for some meaningful identity, some intellectuals moved to Paris and joined the French African advocates of *négritude* whose emphasis on a vague "blackness" or Africanness was primarily a reaction to their assimilation to European culture. With much of their traditional culture destroyed by a colonialism which did little to create a substitute, the African intellectual thus found himself ambivalent toward his traditional culture while being interested in the material aspects of "Western" culture. As such, *négritude* remained highly theoretical and artificial for French and Portuguese African alike.

Confronted by the intransigent policies of the Salazar dictatorship at a time when the tide of independence swept away colonialism and brought nationhood for much of Africa, the intellectuals in Portuguese Africa challenged the assumptions of Lusotropicalism. The African accepted militant and revolutionary alternatives to the independence struggle. His revolution and aspirations for nationhood soon made him aware of the complex structural problems ahead. The nationalist turned to change and development to solve political, economic, social and cultural problems.

Perspectives

The future of Portuguese Africa is dependent in large measure upon developments within the homeland. In 1966 the dictatorship celebrated its fortieth anniversary, although continuity was challenged by the regime's inability to find solutions to the internal and external problems that face all underdeveloped nations. Immobility and stability characterized the political order, which was bolstered by the armed forces and the police, the Catholic Church, and the oligarchy of landowners, industrialists and financiers. There was some evidence of growing dissatisfaction, however, among these supporters as well as anxiety for the aging Salazar, who symbolized resistance to change and structural development. His death or ouster would disrupt the old order and its hegemony over Portuguese society, at which point a coalition of elements might arise to support change and development. (Realistically, this possibility appears unlikely to occur for many years, under any circumstances.)

It could also be argued that the future of the New State is dependent on happenings in Portuguese Africa. Both supporters and adversaries agreed that 1961 was a turning point in the history of Portuguese Africa. Supporters argued that events of that year prompted the regime to consolidate its African position, thereby assuring the continuity of the Lusitanian ideals of community and empire. At the same time an economic and social evolution took place in the overseas territories. Long range construction projects (roads, bridges, and airports) were speeded up to bolster defenses against the warring Africans. Industrial development also increased with the building of new factories, schools, and hospitals. Certain reforms provided the territories with some autonomy, it was argued, while both militarily and economically Portugal's position in Africa was strengthened. Opponents of the regime, however, viewed the continuing guerrilla war as a sign of Portugal's misguided policies and inability to maintain its hold on the overseas territories over the long run.

Emergent nationalism, an extension of earlier tribal resistance to Portuguese rule, challenged the regime in Angola, Portuguese Guiné, and Moçambique. In Angola tens of thousands of Portuguese troops succeeded in reoccupying most of the northern area that had fallen into the hands of rebellious Bacongo elements after the outbreak in early 1961. Only small African resistance was evident in the forested regions. Particularly distressing to the Portuguese was the fact that hundreds of thousands of refugees had fled across the northern border into the Congo. The region was by no means pacified nor fully integrated into the territorial framework. Although the Portuguese welcomed the division of leadership in the nationalist ranks, anxiety and uncertainty characterized their presence not only in the northern area but throughout all Angola. Possible fullscale mobilization of the refugee and indigenous populations into nationalist guerrilla movements was cause for concern. Amalgamation of northern Angola into the Congo itself was a threat contingent not only on Portugal's policy of encouraging tribal divisions but also on political and economic ties with its northern neighbor.

The early success of nationalist guerrilla movements in Guiné augured ill for the Portuguese military force of more than fifteen thousand. Traditionally Guiné was a neglected and weak link in the Portuguese imperial design. Being particularly effective in the dense forests and many waterways, nationalists claimed control over nearly half the territory. Their presence in rural areas caused production declines in agriculture and necessitated increased importation of foodstuffs to supply an apparently demoralized army whose unfamiliarity in a tropical setting was only one reason for concentration in protected rural areas. Nostalgia and patriotic concern constituted the rationale for maintaining a hold on Guiné which had become a liability and a drain on the metropole's human and financial resources.

The Portuguese were pressed to defend Moçambique, where nationalists initiated a guerrilla offensive and achieved moderate success in the northern districts. Although the colony suffered from an annual imbalance of trade, its economic potential was too great to justify abandonment by the Portuguese. Thus a third military front was established to defend the territory from the nationalist challenge. The immediate prospect of partition of the territory appeared unlikely in view of the necessity for neighboring South Africa and Southern Rhodesia to maintain their alliance against the tide of black nationalism. Accordingly, the Salazar regime supported the desire of many Portuguese in Moçambique to seek closer political and economic ties with Pretoria and Salisbury. Recent intensified South African investments in Moçambique and the agreements requiring that a share of South African commerce flow through Lourenço Marques in exchange for African labor suggested that one could not exclude the possibility that white settlers in Moçambique one day might break with Lisbon and align themselves with South Africa.

Two external forces have pressured for an alteration in the stalemate in Portugal and Portuguese Africa. First, the United Nations, influenced by the Afro-Asian bloc of newly independent nations, remain a constant threat to Portuguese rule in Africa. Since 1960 a series of resolutions and reports in the Security Council, in the General Assembly, and in several committees have condemned repressive political, economic, and social conditions in the Portuguese African territories. A second force is represented by the United States, whose policy has favored Portugal and Portuguese Africa. Strong United States pressure on its ally to grant eventual independence to the African colonies could drastically alter the stalemate, however. Salazar might withdraw from NATO, close U.S. military bases in the Açores, and perhaps break diplomatic relations with the United States, but the result could be independence for the African territories.

Bibliographic references are arranged according to subject matter, roughly in the chapter sequence of this book. The evaluative and descriptive comments that follow may assist the reader in examining the primary and secondary sources.

General Portuguese Africa

REFERENCE: A comprehensive listing of Portuguese institutions is included in Centro de Documentação Científica Ultramarina, *Instituições portuguesas de interesse ultramarino* (Lisbon, 1960). Official and unofficial serials published in Portugal and overseas are listed in the Centro's *Periódicos portugueses de interesse ultramarino actualmente em publicação* (Lisbon, 1959). A fairly complete list of studies, papers, and articles prepared under the auspices of the Junta de Investigações do Ultramar, which coordinates most official research projects on Portuguese Africa, is found in Junta das Missões Geográficas de Investigações do Ultramar, Centro de Documentação Científica Ultramarina, *Bibliografica científica da Junta de Investigações do Ultramar*, published annually since 1958. Many of the Junta's publications are in the 1961 catalogue (499 works are listed) of the Agência Geral do Ultramar in Lisbon. Other bibliographies are included in "Bibliografia sôbre economia ultramarina portuguesa," in *Estudos ultramarinos*, 4 (1959), 255-81; José Júlio Gonçalves, "Bibliografia antropológica do Ultramar Português," in *Boletim Geral do Ultramar*, XXXVII (March-April-October-December 1961) *passim*; and J. Lúcio Nunes, *Bibliografia histórico-militar no ultramur Português* (Lisbon, 1965). A synthesis of serial publications, archival material, bibliography, documents, institutions, and political organizations is presented in Ronald H. Chilcote *et al*, "Documenting Portuguese Africa" *Africana Newsletter*, I (Autumn 1963), 16-36.

SERIAL PUBLICATIONS: Among useful publications are *Arquivo das Colónias*, 1917-1931, which reproduces many documents relating to Portuguese Africa; *Boletim Geral do Ultramar*, published under various titles since 1925; *Estudos Ultramarinos*, published quarterly by the Instituto Superior de Estudos Ultramarinos in Lisbon; *Garcia de Orta*, a technical journal of the Junta das Missões Geográficas e de Investigações do Ultramar; *Portugal em Africa*, a Catholic monthly which initiated publication in 1894 and is particularly useful for documentary information on the African resistance and the Portuguese campaigns of pacification; *Studia*, a twice yearly publication of the Centro de

Estudos Históricos Ultramarinos, published since 1958; and *Ultramar: Revista da Comunidade Portuguesa e da Actualidade Ultramarina Internacional,* issued since 1960.

DISCOVERIES, EXPANSION, AND COLONIZATION: For varying views and interpretation on the early centuries of Portuguese activity in Africa, see the writings of the chronicler, Gomes Eannes de Azurara, especially his *Conquests and Discoveries of Henry the Navigator* . . . , (London, 1936); António Baião, Hernâni Cidade, and Manuel Múrias, *História da expansão portuguesa no mundo* (Lisbon, 1937-1940), 3 vols.; João de Barros' classic *Décadas da Asia* (Lisbon, 1945-1946); Raymond C. Beazley, *Prince Henry the Navigator* . . . (New York and London, 1895); John W. Blake, *European Beginnings in West Africa* . . . (London, 1937) and also his *Europeans in West Africa, 1450-1560* (London, 1942), a two-volume set of documents; Damião Peres, *Descobrimentos portugueses* (Oporto, 1943); V. Magalhães Godinho, *Documentos sôbre a expansão portuguesa* (Lisbon, 1943-1956), 3 vols.; A. J. Dinis, *Vida e obras de Gomes Eannes de Zurara* (Lisbon, 1949), 2 vols.; Júlio Gonçalves, *O Infante Dom Pedro, as Sete Partidas e a génese dos descobrimentos* (Lisbon, 1955). Other notable works on the early period are K. G. Jayne, *Vasco da Gama and his Successors* (London, 1910); Richard Henry Major, *The Life of Prince Henry of Portugal* . . . (London, 1868); Centro de Estudos Históricos Ultramarinos, *Documentação ultramarina portuguesa* (Lisbon, 1960), 3 vols., which includes translated documents from the British Museum and other libraries: Edgar Prestage, *The Chronicles of Fernão Lopes and Gomes Eannes de Zurara* . . . (London, 1928) and also his *The Portuguese Pioneers* (London, 1933); and a series of frequently marred studies by Sidney R. Welch, including *Portuguese Rule and Spanish Crown in South Africa, 1581-1640* (Cape Town and Johannesburg, 1950), *South Africa under John III, 1521-1557* (Cape Town and Johannesburg, 1948), and *South Africa under King Manuel, 1495-1521* (Cape Town and Johannesburg, 1946).

Charles R. Boxer, a foremost scholar of Portuguese affairs, surveys the Portuguese colonial experience in a short monograph, *Four Centuries of Portuguese Expansion, 1415-1825: A Succinct Survey* (Johannesburg, 1965). Among his many other outstanding works are *Portuguese Society in the Tropics* . . . (Madison, 1965) and *Salvador de Sá and the Struggle for Brazil and Angola* (London, 1952). Another scholar, Bailey W. Diffie, offers a concise synthesis in his *Prelude to Empire: Portuguese Overseas before Henry the Navigator* (Omaha, 1960). James Duffy's very significant contributions include *Portugal in Africa* (Cambridge, Mass., 1962), *Portuguese Africa* (Cambridge, Mass., 1959), and *The Portuguese African Territories* (Carnegie Endowment for International Peace, 1961). See also Richard Hammond's *Portugal and Africa, 1815-1910* (Stanford, 1966). Eça d'Almeida's *Colonização: um problema nacional* (Lisbon, 1945) analyzes the failures of Portuguese colonization schemes while António da Silva Rêgo's *Portuguese Colonization in the Sixteenth Century* . . . (Johannesburg, 1965) deals with the early history of colonization.

RACE RELATIONS, SLAVERY, AND FORCED LABOR: The view that Portugal never practiced racial discrimination in Africa is upheld by many supporters of New

SUGGESTED READINGS 131

State propaganda, including António Alberto de Andrade, in *Many Races-One Nation. Racial Non-Discrimination always the Cornerstone of Portugal's Overseas Policy* (Lisbon, 1961) and Manuel Dias Belchior, in *Compreendamos os negros!* (Lisbon, 1951). Inherent in the Portuguese literature, however, is the belief that the African Negro is mentally inferior; such a thesis is advocated by Alvaro de Montenegro, *A raça negra perante a civilização* (Lisbon, 1929) and by António F. Nogueira, *A raça negra sob o ponto de vista de civilização da Africa* . . . (Lisbon, 1880). A. A. Mendes Corrêa has contributed two useful studies on racial origin and composition of the peoples of Portuguese Africa: *Raça e nacionalidade* (Rio de Janeiro and Oporto, 1919) and *Raízes de Portugal*, 2d. ed. (Lisbon, 1944). The scholarly writings of Charles R. Boxer place the race question in proper perspective, especially his *Race Relations in the Portuguese Empire, 1415-1825* (Oxford, 1963).

A escravatura . . . (Lisbon, 1944) by Edmundo Correia Lopes focuses on historical developments (1441 to 1850) of the slave trade in the Portuguese African territories. Among Englishmen who accused the Portuguese of labor malpractices were William A. Cadbury, *Labour in Portuguese West Africa*, 2d. ed. (London, 1910); John H. Harris, *Portuguese Slavery: Britain's Dilemma* (London, 1913); and Henry W. Nevinson, *A Modern Slavery* (London, 1906) and *More Changes, More Chances* (London, 1925). The work of an American sociologist, Edward Alsworth Ross, *Report on Employment of Native Labor in Portuguese Africa* (New York, 1925) also was critical of Portuguese labor conditions in Africa. The Portuguese rebuttal to these charges was contained in António A. Corrêa de Aguiar, *O trabalho indígena nas ilhas de São Tomé e Príncipe* (Lisbon, 1910); Francisco Monteiro, *A mão-de-obra em São Tomé e Príncipe* (Lisbon, 1910); and Augusto Ribeiro, *O cacau de São Tomé* . . . (Lisbon, 1910).

An attack on colonial labor conditions in 1947 by Henrique Galvão (see his *Santa Maria: My Crusade for Portugal*, Cleveland and New York, 1961, pp. 57-71) was reiterated a few years later in Basil Davidson's *The African Awakening* (London, 1955). The rejoinder to Davidson's attack came from an English apologist for the Salazar regime, F. C. C. Egerton, in *Angola without Prejudice* (Lisbon, 1955). Working conditions in Portuguese Africa were also the subject of a useful report by the International Labour Organisation in its *Official Bulletin*, XLV (April 1962), Supplement II, 1-253.

POLICY AND STRUCTURAL PROBLEMS: For material on the politics of the New State regime see: Michael Derrick's *The Portugal of Salazar* (London, 1938), a sympathetic but detailed account of the regime's early years; F. C. C. Egerton's apologetic *Salazar, Rebuilder of Portugal* (London, 1943); António Ferro's *Salazar: Portugal and her Leader* (London, 1939); and José H. Saraiva's *Accão e doutrinação* (Lisbon, 1958). Salazar's public writings and speeches are included in *Discursos e notas políticas* (Coimbra, 1935-1959, 5 vols.). Recommended from the prolific Portuguese literature on New State colonial administrative policy and doctrine are Joaquim da Silva Cunha's *O sistema português de política indígena* (Coimbra, 1953) and *O trabalho indígena: estudo de direito colonial* (Lisbon, 1954); Osvaldo Aguiar's *Velhas e novas estructuras no ultramar português* (Lisbon, 1964); Avila de Azevedo's *Política de ensino em Africa* (Lisbon, 1958); Manuel Dias Belchior's *A missão de Portugal em*

Africa (Lisbon, 1960); and Armindo Monteiro's *Para uma política imperial* (Lisbon, 193?). On the now abrogated native statute, see chapter XVIII in António Joaquim Alfaro's *Angola, Your Neighbor*, 1950 (Lisbon, 1950) and Vasco Soares da Veiga, *Estatutos dos indígenas portugueses das provincias* . . . (Lisbon, 1957). Richard Pattee apologetically reviews Portuguese metropolitan and overseas doctrine and policy in *Portugal na Africa contemporânea* (Coimbra, 1959) and in *Portugal and the Portuguese World* (Milwaukee, 1957). In "Portuguese Roots in Africa," *Optima*, XV (March 1965), 1-15, Austin Coates offers a sympathetic view of the contemporary situation. James Duffy presents an objective but critical analysis of administrative policy in chapters IX to XIII of his *Portuguese Africa*. Critical analyses are also included in António de Figueiredo's *Portugal and Its Empire: The Truth* (London, 1961); Peter Fryer and Patricia McGowan Pinheiro's *Oldest Ally: A Portrait of Salazar's Portugal* (London, 1961); and in Perry Anderson's *Le Portugal et la fin de l'ultracolonialisme* (Paris, 1963), which incorporates three articles appearing in *New Left Review* during 1962.

Critics of the regime and its overseas policy include Francisco da Cunha Leal, a longtime opponent of Salazar, who published a devastating attack on colonial policy in his *Oliveira Salazar, filomeno da câmara e o império colonial português* (Lisbon, 1930) and in two recent books, *A gadanha da morte: reflexões sôbre os problemas euro-africanos* (Lisbon, 1961) and *A pátria em perigo* (Lisbon, 1962). A former Salazar supporter, Manuel José Homem de Mello, offered his suggestions for colonial policy in *Portugal, o ultramar e o futuro* (Lisbon, 1962). Critical of Cunha Leal and Homem de Mello's views as well as official policy, Fernando Pacheco de Amorim polemically argues for "integration" of the overseas provinces in *Três caminhos da política ultramarina* (Coimbra, 1962) and *Unidade ameaçada: o problema ultramarino* (Coimbra, 1963).

For the economic theory of the corporative system, see Marcello Caetano's *A obra financeira de Salazar* (Lisbon, 1934), *O sistema corporativo* (Lisbon, 1938), and *Problemas da revolução corporativa* (Lisbon, 1941); José Pires Cardoso's *Para uma corporação autêntica* (Lisbon, 1958); Freppel Cotta's *Economic Planning in Corporative Portugal* (London, 1937); Mário Pinto dos Santos Martins' *Organização corporativa* (Lisbon, 1960?); Mário Morais de Oliveira's *Aspectos actuais do corporativismo perante a vida económica* (Lisbon, 1958); Pedro Teotónio Pereira's *A batalha do futuro: organização corporativa* (Lisbon, 1937), Salazar's *O trabalho e as corporações no pensamento de Salazar* (Lisbon, 196?); and George S. West's *The New Corporative State of Portugal* (Lisbon, 1937). See also the two volume bibliography by A. D. Guerreiro, *Bibliografia sôbre a economia portuguesa* (Lisbon, 1958).

For details on economic planning in Portugal and in overseas Africa, see *Projecto de plano de fomento para 1959-1964* (Lisbon, 1958) and *Projecto de plano intercolar de fomento para 1965-1967* (Lisbon, 1964). Also two official studies issued by the Secretariado Nacional da Informação entitled *The Portuguese Economic Development Drive* (Lisbon, n.d.) and *Aspects of the Portuguese Economy* (Lisbon, 1963). The survey by W. W. McVittie, *Portugal: Economic and Commercial Conditions* . . . (London, 1955) contains useful but dated information which may be supplemented by the annual survey of economic conditions issued by the Organisation for Economic Co-operation and Development. See also the very useful analysis by V. Xavier Pintado, *Structure and Growth of the Portuguese Economy* (Geneva, 1964). Cunha Leal's criticism of Salazar's financial policy and the economy in general is contained in his *A obra intangível do dr. Oliveira Salazar* (Lisbon, 1930); *História do conflicto entre um ministro das finanças e um governador do Banco de Angola* (Lisbon, 1930); and *Peregrinações através do poder económico* (Lisbon, 1960). Less polemical and very important are works by Salazar supporters and leading economists, including Luís Maria Teixeira Pinto's *Alguns aspectos da teoria do crescimento económico* (Lisbon, 1956) and Pereira de Moura and Teixeira Pinto's *Problemas do crescimento económico português* (Lisbon, 1958).

On economic conditions in the African territories, see the incisive analysis by Richard J. Hammond, *Portugal's African Problem: Some Economic Facets,* issued as an occasional paper by the Carnegie Endowment for International Peace in New York, 1962; also Hammond's "Economic Imperialism, Sidelights on a Stereotype," *The Journal of Economic History,* XXI (December 1961), 582-98; Jorge E. da Costa Oliveira, *Aplicação de capitais nas províncias ultramarinas* (Lisbon, 1961); and a Harvard University doctoral dissertation by Roberto S. de Medeiros Fernandes, "Portugal and its Overseas Territories: Economic Structure and Policies" (Cambridge, Mass., 1960); and the two-part study of the United Nations' special committee on colonialism, "The Activities of Foreign Economic and other Interests which are Impeding the Implementation of the Declaration on the Granting of Independence in the Territories under Portuguese Administration" (New York, 1965). The quarterly *Boletim Trimestral* of the Banco Nacional Ultramarino provides useful information and data.

Portugal's attempt to control social and cultural life at home and in the colonies is the subject of J. Pires Cardoso's *Uma escola corporativa portuguesa* (Lisbon, 1949) and *A universidade instituição corporativa* (Lisbon, 1952). More critical of social and cultural problems are Vidal Caldas Nogueira, *O estado da cultura e do civismo português* (Oporto, 1948) and António Sérgio, *Educação cívica* (Lisbon, 1954) and *A short Survey of Social Assistance Work in Portugal (1128-1945)* (Lisbon, 1945). Also see the article by Buango Fele (pseudonym for Mário de Andrade), "Crise de l'ensignement dans les colonies portugaises," in *Présence Africaine,* 7 (April-May 1956), 85-93; and Michael H. Higgins and Charles F. S. de Winton, *Survey of Education in Portugal* (London, 1942).

INSTITUTIONAL FORCES: There is very little literature on institutional forces, with the exception of the Catholic Church. Useful works on the Church include Fortunato de Almeida's classic eight-volume *História da igreja em Portugal* (Coimbra, 1910-1917) and P. Miguel de Oliveira's *História eclesiástica de Portugal* (Lisbon, 1958); Salazar's brief *Centro católica português* (Coimbra, 1922) which reveals his early ties to the Church: J. Pires Cardoso's *O corporativismo e a igreja* (Lisbon, 1949), a pamphlet explaining the Church's role in the corporative structure; and Paul Blanshard's *Freedom and Catholic Power in Spain and Portugal: An American Interpretation* (Boston, 1962), especially pages 195-266 which criticize the Church and the New State. Historical notes and documents are in Canon Eurico Nogueira's *Church and State in Portugal* (Lisbon, n.d.). The reference work edited by Albano Mendes Pedro, *Anuário católico do ultramar português*, provides a useful breakdown of Catholic missionary activities in the overseas territories. Other important general works on missionary activities in Africa are José Júlio Gonçalves' two volume *Protestantismo em Africa* (Lisbon, 1960) and António da Silva Rêgo's *Alguns problemas sociológico-missionários da Africa negra* (Lisbon, 1960), *Curso de missionologia* (Lisbon, 1956), and *Lições de missionologia* (Lisbon, 1961). On the military, Fernando Queiroga's *Portugal oprimido* (Rio de Janeiro, 1958) and Humberto Delgado's *The Memoirs of General Delgado* (London, 1964) and *Tufão sôbre Portugal* (Rio de Janeiro, 1962) deal with life under the New State and the attempts by the authors to overthrow the regime. Other works, all polemical, are Amílcar Gomes Duarte's *A resistência em Portugal: crônicas* (São Paulo, 1962) about the activities of the secret police; the International Union of Students' *The Case Against Salazar: Report on Portugal* (Prague, 1963?) which attempts to document the student protests of 1962 and thereafter; Alexandre Vieira's *Figuras grada do movimento social português* (Lisbon, 1959), a collection of biographies and excerpts from the writings of labor figures; Luís Portela and Edgart Rodrigues' *Na inquisição do Salazar* (Rio de Janeiro, 1957), which traces the history of the workers' movement and its suppression; and Carlos Pereira's *Fala um lavrador* (Lisbon, 1960), a critique of rural manual field laborers' conditions.

NATIONALISM AND DEVELOPMENT: A number of basic works can be consulted to support theoretical assumptions relating to nationalism and developmental nationalism. Among the most useful are Karl W. Deutsch, *Nationalism and Social Communications* (Cambridge, Mass., 1953); Rupert Emerson, *From Empire to Nation* (Cambridge, Mass., 1960); Edward Shils, *Political Development in the New States* (London, 1965); and K. H. Silvert (ed.), *Expectant Peoples: Nationalism and Development* (New York, 1963), especially the appendix of propositions and hypotheses. Deutsch's *An Interdisciplinary Bibliography on Nationalism, 1933-1953* (Cambridge, Mass., 1956) is a basic, though dated, reference work. Among helpful articles are Leonard Binder, "National Integration and Political Development," *American Political Science Review*, LVIII (September 1964), 622-31; James S. Coleman, "Nationalism in Tropical Africa," *American Political Science Review*, XLVIII (June 1954), 404-26; and Deutsch's "The Growth of Nations: Some Recurrent Patterns of Political and Social Integration," in *World Politics*, V (January 1953), 168-95, and his "Social Mobilization and Political Development," in *American Political Science Review*, LV (September 1961), 493-514.

There is much material on Portuguese nationalism, imperial destiny, and colonial mystique. Both the Portuguese critic, Fidelino de Figueiredo and the British critic, Aubrey F. B. Bell, offer incisive views of Portuguese character and behavior, respectively in *Cáracteristicas da litteratura portuguesa* (Lisbon, 1923) and *In Portugal* (London, 1911?), particularly in chapter 1. See also V. de Bragança-Cunha's interesting *Eight Centuries of Portuguese Monarchy* . . . (London, 1911) and *Revolutionary Portugal* (London, 1937). Dan Stanislawsky in his scholarly monograph, *The Individuality of Portugal* (Austin, 1959), analyzes the roots of Portuguese nationalism from a geographical point of view. Alexandre Herculano in his *História de Portugal* (Paris and Lisbon, 1914-1916) rebuts the thesis that Portuguese nationalism evolved from the Lusitanian resistance to the Romans. Norton de Matos, a former governor of Angola, in *A nação uma . . .* (Lisbon, 1953?) offers suggestions for implementing traditional colonial policy. The relationship of policy to nationalism is stated in legislative documents: *Political Constitution of the Portuguese Republic* (Lisbon, 1957) which incorporates in pp. 36-44 Salazar's Colonial Act; and *Organic Law of the Portuguese Overseas Provinces* (Lisbon, 1963), the reform legislation enacted under Adriano Moreira. Salazar defends his policies in a collection of essays entitled *The Road for the Future* (Lisbon, 1963) and in a series of speeches and interviews: "Portugal and the Anti-Colonialist Campaign" (Lisbon, 1960), "The Portuguese Overseas Territories and the United Nations Organization," (Lisbon, 1961); "Appeal to the People" (Lisbon, 1961); "Portuguese Problems in Africa" (Lisbon, 1962); and "Declaration on Overseas Policy" (Lisbon, 1963); as well as an article, "Realities and Trends of Portugal's Policies" in *International Affairs* (London), XXIX (April 1963), 169-83. Moreira's views appear in his *Portugal's Stand in Africa* (New York, 1962) and in *Partido Português* (Lisbon, 1962?) and earlier thoughts in *Ensaios* (Lisbon, 1960). A longtime Salazar supporter, António Júlio de Castro Fernandes, writes on the Portuguese mystical conception of the "Nation" in a pamphlet, *The Presence of the Portuguese in Africa* (Lisbon, 1961). Luís C. Lupi in *Portugal and her Overseas Provinces* (Lisbon, 1961) also analyzes and defends policy. Two other important Portuguese statements are Marcello Caetano's *Portugal e a internacionalização dos problemas africanos* (Lisbon, 1963) and Franco Nogueira's *The United Nations and Portugal: A Study of Anti-Colonialism* (London, 1963).

Gilberto Freyre introduces the concept of Lusotropicology in *Um brasileiro em terras portuguêsas* (Rio de Janeiro, 1953). His later ideas are delineated in several studies published by the Portuguese government, including *The Portuguese and the Tropics* (Lisbon, 1961) and *Portuguese Integration in the Tropics* (Lisbon, 1961); also in an interesting article, "Misconceptions of Brazil," in *Foreign Affairs*, XL (April 1962), 453-62. The Freyre thesis is the basis for much debate among Portuguese, Brazilians, and Africans. The Portuguese position is portrayed in Jorge Dias' *Ensaios etnológicos* (Lisbon, 1961); in Lobiano do Rego's *Pátria morena: a vista da maior epoeia* (Lisbon, 1959); and in the Centro de Estudos Políticos e Sociais' *Colóquios sôbre problemas humanos nas regiões tropicais* (Lisbon, 1961). Freyre's thesis is challenged by the Brazilian historian, José Honório Rodrigues, in *Brazil e Africa: outro horizonte* (Rio de Janeiro, 1961 and 1964) and in a two-part series, "O presente e o futuro das relações africano-brasileiras," in *Revista Brasileira de Política Internacional*, V (June 1962), 263-84 and V (September 1962), 501-516. Rodrigues' Brazilian nationalist view is presented also in "The Influence of Africa on Brazil and of Brazil on Africa," in *Journal of African History*, III, 1 (1962), 49-67. Roger Bastide critically reviewed Rodrigues' book in *Présence Africaine*, English ed., XIII, 41 (1962), 90-95. Bastide also contributed a related article "Variations on Négritude," to *Pré-*

sence Africaine, English ed., VIII (First Quarter 1961), 83-92. Other Brazilian views on Lusotropicology and Portuguese and Brazilian policy in Africa appear in a prolific literature on the subject; recommended are Vamireh Chacon's *A revolução no trópico* (Rio de Janeiro, 1962), Jarbas Maranhão's *Brasil-Africa: um mesmo caminho* (São Paulo, 1962), Cândido António Mendes de Almeida's *Nacionalismo e desenvolvimento* (Rio de Janeiro, 1963), and Adolpho Justo Beserra de Menezes' *O Brazil e o mundo asio-africano* (Rio de Janeiro, 1960).

Writing under the pseudonym, Buanga Fele, the Angolan Mário de Andrade attacks the Freyre thesis in "Qu'est-ce que le 'luso tropicalismo'?" in *Présence Africaine*, New Series, French ed., 4 (October-November 1955), 24-35; this is the most definitive statement expressing the African criticism of Lusotropicology. Andrade also analyzes the meaning and significance of Angolan nationalism in "El nacionalismo angolés," *Tribuna Socialista*, 6-7 (February- May 1963), 26-34 and in a collection of essays entitled *Liberté pour l'Angola* (Paris, 1962). Eduardo Mondlane treats nationalism in a mimeographed eleven-page statement, "The Development of Nationalism in Mozambique," (Dar es Salaam, December 3, 1964). Hundreds of ephemeral sources on nationalism written by Andrade, Mondlane, and other African leaders are included in the present author's personal collection and will be cited in an extensive bibliography to a book of documents entitled *Emerging Nationalism in Portuguese Africa* (forthcoming).

Angola

John W. Blake in *European Beginnings in West Africa* . . . has included an excellent bibliography of both documentary and general materials. The bibliography by Paul Borchardt, *Bibliographie de l'Angola, 1500-1910* (Brussels, 1912?) focuses on historical and economic geography.

Among the important contributions by Portuguese writers are: Ralph Delgado, *História de Angola, 1482-1836*, 4 vols. (Benguela, 1948-55) and *Ao sul do Cuanza*, 2 vols. (Lisbon, 1940); Hélio A. Esteves Felgas, *História do Congo Português* (Carmona, 1958); Alfredo de Albuquerque Felner, *Angola* . . . (Coimbra, 1933), including a useful appendix of documents; J. C. Feo Cardozo de Castellobranco e Torres, *Memorias contendo a biographia do vice almirante Luiz da Motta Feo e Torres. A história dos governadores e capitaens generães de Angola, desde 1575 até 1825* . . . (Paris, 1825); Alberto Lemos, *História de Angola, 1482-1684* (Lisbon, 1932); Duarte Lopes, *A Report of the Kingdom of Congo* . . . (London, 1881), an important narrative of the early colonial period; António de Oliveira de Cadornega, *História geral das guerras angolanas*, 3 vols. (Lisbon, 1940-42), a significant work despite some erroneous interpretation; Visconde de Paiva Manso, *História do Congo (Documentos)* (Lisbon, 1877), an invaluable work; Elias Alexandre da Silva Corrêa, *História da Angola* (Lisbon, 1937), a reprint of a late eighteenth century writing.

Useful Portuguese writings on the native Angolan include: Ivo Benjamin de Cerqueira, *Vida social indígena na colónia de Angola (usos e costumes)* (Lisbon, 1947); Carlos Estermann, *Etnografia do sudoeste de Angola*, 2 vols., (Lisbon, 1956-57); Hélio A. Esteves Felgas, *As populações nativas do congo português* (Luanda, 1960); Luís Figueira, *Africa banto: raças e tribos de Angola* (Lisbon, 1938); Serra Frazão, *Associações secretas entre os indígenas de Angola* (Lisbon, 1946); and Mário Milheiros, *Etnografia angolana . . .* (Luanda, 1951).

Among useful contributions by foreign writers are: Alexander T. Barnes, *Angolan Sketches* (London, 1928), a general narrative; Andrew Battel, *The Strange Adventures of Andrew Battel of Leigh, in Angola . . .* edited with notes and a concise history by Ernst George Ravenstein (London, 1901); David Birmingham, *The Portuguese Conquest of Angola* (London, 1965) and also his *Trade and Conflict in Angola: The Mbundu . . . 1483-1790* (London, 1966); Charles R. Boxer, *Salvador de Sá and the Struggle for Brazil and Angola, 1602-1686* (London, 1952); Gladwyn Murray Childs, *Umbundu Kinship and Character . . .* (London, 1949), including an important chapter on historical developments in Benguela; Mary Cushman, *Missionary Doctor: The Story of Twenty Years in Angola* (New York, 1944); Adrian C. Edwards, *The Ovimbundu under Two Sovereignties . . .* (London, 1962); John T. Tucker, *Angola, the Land of the Blacksmith Prince* (London, 1933); and Douglas L. Wheeler, "The Portuguese in Angola, 1836-1891 . . ." (Ph.D. Dissertation, Boston University, 1963).

A defense of Portugal in Angola is contained in *Angola, curso de extensão universitária* (Lisbon, 1963?), a collection of essays by Portuguese specialists; Augusto Casimiro, *Angola e o futuro* (Lisbon, 1958); Domingos da Cruz, *A crise de Angola* (Lisbon, 1928); Vicente Ferreira, *A política colonial portuguesa em Angola* (Coimbra, 1932); Gil Marçal, *Angola: ponto fulcral da nação portuguesa* (Oporto, 1947); José Norton de Matos, *Memórias e trabalhos da minha vida*, 4 vols., (Lisbon, 1945-46) as well as his *A província de Angola* (Oporto, 1926); and Henrique de Paiva Couceiro, *Angola . . .* (Lisbon, 1910).

With renewed African resistance and rebellion in 1961, a flurry of polemical and patriotic books appeared, including: Horácio Caio, *Angola: os dias do desespero,* (Lisbon, 1961); Amândio César, *Angola 1961* (Lisbon, 1961); Gonçalves Cotta, *Grito de Angola . . .* (Luanda, 1961); Hélio Esteves Felgas, *Guerra em Angola* (Lisbon, 1962); Artur Maciel, *Angola heróica . . .* (Lisbon, 1963); Alves Pinheiro, *Angola . . .* (Rio de Janeiro, 1961); Pedro Pires *et al, Braseiro da morte . . .* (Viseu, 1963); Bernardo Teixeira, *The Fabric of Terror . . .* (New York, 1965); and *Angola, terra nossa* (Lisbon, 1962).

The writings of two Portuguese critics of policy in Angola, Henrique Galvão and Manuel Vinhas, include the former's *Outras terras, outras gentes . . .* (Lisbon, 1941) and *Por Angola . . .* (Lisbon, n.d.) and the latter's *Aspectos actuais de Angola* (Lisbon, 1961) and *Para um diálogo sôbre Angola* (Lisbon, 1962). David Magno has written a brief history of the native resistance to the Portuguese from 1915-1919 in his *Guerras angolanas* (Oporto, 1934).

The African native view of conditions in the Portuguese territories is found in some of the documents contained in *Angola: através dos textos* (São Paulo, 1962); and in various issues of *Présence Africaine,* including "Angola Casebook," XVII, 45 (First quarter 1963), 151-96 and a special issue on Angola in XIV/XV, 42/43 (1962), 1-208. Useful also for understanding the African's outlook are Mário de Andrade's *Antologia da poesia negra de expressão por-*

tuguesa (Paris, 1955); Costa Andrade's *Tempo angolano em Italia: poemas* (São Paulo, 1963); and Merlin Ennis, *Umbundu Folk Tales from Angola* (Boston, 1962).

For foreign works by non-Portuguese writers concerned with the African's struggle for independence and the failure of Portuguese policy, see Len Addicott, *Cry Angola* (London, 1962); Robert Davezies, *Les Angolais* (Paris, 1965), which includes interviews with nationalist leaders and interpretation of nationalist activities; Basil Davidson, *Angola, 1961* (London, 1961); Anders Ehnmark and Per Wästberg, *Angola and Mozambique: The Case Against Portugal* (London, 1963); Institute of Race Relations, *Angola: A symposium* (New York, 1962); Homer Jack, *Angola: Repression and Revolt in Portuguese Africa* (New York, 1960); Thomas Okuma, *Angola in Ferment* . . . (Boston, 1962); and K. Madhu Panikkar, *Angola in Flames* (New York, 1962).

Portuguese Guiné, São Tomé and Príncipe,
and the Cape Verde Archipelago

Among the early Portuguese chronicles and writings are André Alvares d'Aldama, *Tratado breve dos rios Guiné do Cabo Verdi desde o rio de Sanagá até aos baixos de Sant'Anna* . . . *1954* (Oporto, 1841); Gomes Eannes de Azurara, *Discovery and Conquest of Guinea*, translated and edited by E. Prestage and C. R. Beazley, 2 vols., (London, 1896-99); Francisco de Lemos Coelho, *Duas descrições seiscentistas da Guiné* (Lisbon, 1953), which comprises two unedited seventeenth-century manuscripts; and Th. Monod, Avelino Teixeira da Mota, and R. Mauny, *Description de la côte occidentale d'Afrique par Valentim Fernandes (1506-1510)* (Bissau, 1951). A detailed description is in José Conrado Carlos de Chelmicki, *Corografia cabo-verdiana, ou descripção geographico-histórica da provincia das ilhas de Cabo Verde e Guiné* (Lisbon, 1841). João Barreto's *História da Guiné 1418-1918* (Lisbon, 1938) includes extensive quotations from primary sources. Another useful and detailed secondary source is Christiano José de Senna Barcellos, *Subsídios para a história de Cabo Verde e Guiné* . . . , 5 vols. (Lisbon, 1899-1911).

Among other Portuguese sources are Armando de Aguiar, *Guiné, minha terra* (Lisbon, 1964); António Almada Negreiros, *Colonies portugaises: île de San-Thomé avec cartes* (Paris, 1901); Henrique Dias de Carvalho, *Guiné* . . . (Lisbon, 1944), comprising notes of a nineteenth century colonial administrator; Augusto Casimiro, *Portugal Crioulo* (Lisbon, 1940), a narrative of life and customs in the Cape Verdes; A. A. Mendes Corrêa, *Ultramar português, II: Ilhas de Cabo Verde* (Lisbon, 1954), an official detailed account; José Júlio Gonçalves, *O islamismo na Guiné Portuguesa* . . . (Lisbon, 1961); Avelino Teixeira da Mota, *Topónimos de origem portuguesa na costa ocidental de Africa desde o Cabo Bojador ao Cabo de Santa Caterina* (Bissau, 1950), and also the two-volume *Guiné Portuguesa* (Lisbon, 1954), both useful reference works by a specialist on Guiné; Sarmento Rodrigues, *No governo da Guiné* (Lisbon, 1952), memoirs of an administrator; Ernesto J. de C. e Vasconcellos, *Colónias portuguesas, Is Archipelago de Cabo Verde* . . . (Lisbon, 1916) and *Colónias portuguesas, II: Guiné Portuguesa* . . . (Lisbon, 1917); and Luís António de Carvalho Viegas, *Guiné Portuguesa*, 2 vols. (Lisbon, 1936, 1939), being the memoirs of a former governor.

Three useful but dated monographs by the Great Britain Foreign Office are *Cape Verde Islands* (London, 1920), *Portuguese Guinea* (London, 1920), and *San Thomé and Príncipe* (London, 1920).

The Centro de Estudos da Guiné Portuguesa in Bissau has published a series of ethnographic studies, among which are António Carreira, *Mandingas da Guiné Portuguesa* (Bissau, 1947); *Fulas do Gabú* (Bissau, 1948); Augusto J. Santos Lima, *Organização económica e social dos Bijagós* (Bissau, 1947); and Artur Augusto da Silva, *Usos e costumes jurídicos dos Fulas da Guiné Portuguesa* (Bissau, 1958). On Cape Verde, there are *Colóquios Cabo-verdianos* (Lisbon, 1959) and Almerindo Lessa and Jacques Ruffié *Seroantropologia das ilhas de Cabo Verde . . .* (Lisbon, 1957), both of which tend to support theories of Lusotropicology. Also useful are the descriptive account of Archibald Lyall in *Black and White Make Brown . . .* (London, 1938) and António Almada Negreiros, *História ethnographica da ilha de S. Thomé* (Lisbon, 1895).

The writings of Teixeira da Mota and other Portuguese specialists are also found in an important journal, *Boletim Cultural da Guiné Portuguesa*, which was first issued in 1946. Amílcar Cabral, a Cape Verdean agronomist also contributed important writings to that journal, including the very important "Recenseamento agrícola da Guiné: estimativa em 1953" in *Boletim . . . ,* XI (July 1956), 7-243. Some of Cabral's early writings are also found in *Cabo Verde: Boletim de Propaganda e Informação*, an official monthly bulletin first issued in October 1949. Cabral's nationalist writings have appeared in mimeographed form, issued by his Partido Africano da Independência da Guiné e Cabo Verde. For details on the nationalist movement see Gérard Chaliand, *Guinée "portugaise" et Cap Vert en lutte pour leur indépendance* (Paris, 1964).

Moçambique

General bibliographies on Moçambique include Felipe Gastão de Almeida de Eça, *Achegas para a bibliografia de Moçambique . . .* (Lisbon, 1946). The reader should also consult the excellent appendices and bibliographies in Eric Axelson's major works (see below).

Essential documentation for the study of Moçambican history is in *Documentos sôbre os portugueses em Moçambique e na Africa Central . . .* 3 vols. (Lisbon, 1962); A. C. P. Gamitto, *King Kazembe*, translated by Ian Cunnison, (Lisbon, 1960); Francisco Santana, *Documentação avulsa moçambicana do archivo histórico ultramarino* (Lisbon, 1964); and João dos Santos, *Ethiopia oriental e varia história de cousas notaveis do oriente* (Evora, 1609). Also useful are specialized articles in the official quarterly, *Moçambique*, which commenced publication in Lourenço Marques in 1933.

General Portuguese writings include: Sarmento Rodrigues, *Presença de Moçambique na vida da nação . . .* (Lisbon, 1965); António de Almada Negreiros, *Le Mozambique . . .* (Paris, 1904), a general survey; Eugénio Ferreira de Almeida, *Governo do distrito de Moçambique . . .* (Nampula, 1957); Alexandre Lobato, *Evolução administrativa e económica de Moçambique, 1752-1763* (Lisbon, 1957) and also his *A expansão portuguesa em Moçambique de 1498 a 1530*, 3 vols., (Lisbon, 1954-60); Oliveira Boléo,

Moçambique (Lisbon, 1951); J. Guedes da Silva, *Colonização fomento e nacionalização de Moçambique* (Lourenço Marques, 1928); and Ernesto de Vilhena, *Regime dos prazos da Zambézia* . . . (Lisbon, 1916). The bishop of Beira, Sebastião Soares de Resende has mildly criticized Portuguese policy in *Por um Moçambique melhor* (Lisbon, 1963) and *Projeção do natal em Africa* (Lisbon, 1963).

Portuguese writings on ethnography include *Portuguese Contribution to Cultural Anthropology* (Johannesburg, 1964), a study of the Maconde of northern Moçambique by Jorge A. Dias, and *Raças e linguas indígenas em Moçambique* . . . (Lourenço Marques, 1905) by Ayres d'Ornellas. Among the important Portuguese writings of native resistance to the Portuguese in Moçambique are: Agência Geral das Colónias, *As campanhas de Moçambique em 1895* (Lisbon, 1947); Felipe Gastão de Almeida de Eça, *História das guerras no Moçambique: Chicoa e Massangano* (1807-1888), 2 vols. (Lisbon, 1953); Alfredo César Brandão, *A conferência do Snr. Paiva de Andrade acerca da recente campanha que poz termo ao domínio do Bonga na Zambézia* (Lisbon, 1888); António Ennes, *A guerra de Africa em 1895* . . . (Lisbon, 1945) and *Moçambique* . . . 2d. ed., (Lisbon, 1946); Joaquim Mousinho de Albuquerque, *Mousinho de Albuquerque*, 2 vols., 2d. ed., (Lisbon, 1934-35) and *A prisão do Gungunhana* . . . (Lisbon, 1896); Ayres d'Ornellas, *Campanha do Gungunhana, 1895*, 2d. ed., (Lisbon, 1930) and *Colectanea das suas principais obras militares e coloniais*, 2 vols., 2d. ed., (Lisbon, 1934); J. C. Paiva de Andrade, *Campanhas da Zambézia* . . . (Lisbon, 1887); Agência Geral das Colónias, *As campanhas de Moçambique em 1895 segundo os contemporaneos* (Lisbon, 1947); and José Justino Teixeira Botelho, *História militar e política dos portugueses em Moçambique de 1833 aos nossos dias*, 2d. ed. (Lisbon, 1936).

Eric Axelson in *Portuguese in South-east Africa, 1600-1700* (Johannesburg, 1960) and in *South-east Africa, 1488-1530* (London, 1940) has given us two significant historical contributions. Among other non-Portuguese writings are Charles R. Boxer and Carlos de Azevedo, *Fort Jesus and the Portuguese in Mombasa, 1593-1729* (London, 1960); Ralph von Gersdorff, *Moçambique* (Bonn, 1958); Genesta Hamilton, *In the Wake of da Gama; the Story of Portuguese Pioneers in East Africa, 1497-1729*, (London, 1951); Robert Nuñez Lyne, *Mozambique* . . . (London, 1913); Eduardo Moreira, *Portuguese East Africa: a Study of its Religious Needs* (London, 1936); Justus Strandes, *The Portuguese Period in East Africa* (Nairobi, 1961); P. R. Warhurst, *Anglo-Portuguese Relations in South-Central Africa, 1890-1900* (London, 1962); and William Basil Worsfold, *Portuguese Nyassaland* . . . (London, 1899). C. P. Spence surveys the Moçambique economy in *Moçambique: East African Province of Portugal* (Cape Town, 1963) which updates an earlier study, *The Portuguese Colony of Mozambique: An Economic Survey* (Cape Town, 1951). Edwin S. Munger in "Mozambique: Uneasy Today, Uncertain Tomorrow" (New York, American University Field Staff Reports, 1961) reviews political prospects for the territory, and Marvin Harris in *Portugal's African "Wards"* (New York, 1960) offers a critique of Portuguese labor practices.

Three official British studies are useful, especially *A Manual of Portuguese East Africa* (London, 1920), an excellent reference source even though it is dated; also *Mozambique* (London, 1920) and J. M. Bryce Nairn, *Portuguese East Africa (Mozambique): Economic and Commercial Conditions* (London, 1955).

Most useful of the writings of African nationalists are Frente de Libertação de Moçambique (FRELIMO), *First Congress-Documents* (Paris, 1962); the speeches and writings of Eduardo Mondlane, including "The Movement for Freedom in Mozambique," a mimeographed paper delivered in Florence, Italy, in June 1964; Mozambique National Democratic Union, *The* UDEN-AMO *at the United Nations* (Cairo, 1963) and also its *Constitution and Programme* (Cairo, 1963?). Other information is found in the FRELIMO's mimeographed bulletins, *Boletim de Informação, Boletim Nacional,* and *Mozambican Revolution,* all issued in Dar es Salaam.

INDEX

Abako party, 57
Abreu e Brito, Domingos, 67
Açores, 3, 4, 21, 41
Aden, 6
Adoula, Cyrille, 81
Affonso I (Mbemba a Nzinga), 7, 62, 63, 64
African Liberation Committee, 79
Ajáuas tribe, 108, 118
Albuquerque, Affonso de, 6
Albuquerque, Mousinho de, 15, 117
Alcáçer-Kebir, 9, 87
Algeria, 77, 121
Aliança Zombo, 79-80
Almeida, Francisco de, 5, 6, 67
Alvaro I, King of Congo, 64
Alvaro II, King of Congo, 67
Alvaro IV, King of Congo, 69
Amatonga tribe, 109
Ambo tribe, 56, 58
Amorim, Pacheco de, 18-19
Andrade, Mário de, 30, 50, 79
Angola, 1, 5, 7, 53-83, 136-138
    African refugees, 55, 59-60
    Catholic Church, 55, 57, 58, 59, 63, 67, 80
    conquest of, 7, 10, 53, 58, 63-74
    economic conditions, 24, 60-61
    education, 58-59
    ethnic groups, 55-58
    geography, 53, 55, 57, 58
    labor, 61, 75-76
    Nationalist movements, 7, 21, 40, 50, 52, 53, 75-81
    pacification, 53, 59-60, 71, 75-76
    Portuguese emigration, 56, 61
    Primavera, outbreak at, 76
    Protestant influence, 7, 55, 57, 58-59
    resistance, 21, 53, 63-74, 77
    slavery, 7, 11-12, 55-56, 62-63, 77
Angola Diamond Company, 24

Angola Mining Company, 60
Angola Negra, 78
Angonia, 117, 119
Angónis tribe, 110, 115
António I, King of Congo, 65
António III, King of Congo, 7, 80
Anzico tribe, 63
Arguim, 4, 11, 87
Ari Kiluanje, 69
Assimilation policy, 15-17, 27, 29, 49, 51
Associação Africana (Moçambique), 50, 119
Associação Africana do Sul de Angola, 78
Associação dos Naturais de Moçambique, 119
Associação Regional dos Naturais de Angola, 50, 77-78, 119
Avante, 78
Axim, 4, 87
Azurara, Gomes Eannes de, 3, 86

Bacongo, 81
Bafatá, 83, 85, 97
Bailundo kingdom, 57, 72, 73, 74, 75
Baiote tribe, 89, 90, 98
Balanta tribe, 89, 90, 91, 96, 98, 101, 102
Bambadinca, 97, 101
Banhai tribe, 109, 110
Banhun tribe, 89
Bantu, 56, 108, 109, 112
Banyans, 108
Barbosa, Rafael, 100
Barreto, Honório Pereira, 88
Barué, 109, 117
Bassarel, 94, 98
Beafada tribe, 89, 90, 94, 95
Beaver, Philip, 88
Beira, 55, 107, 117
Benguela, 7, 11, 53, 56, 57, 68, 71
Bié kingdom, 71, 72, 73, 74, 75, 78

Bijagós archipelago, 83, 98
  tribe, 89, 90, 91, 94
Bissau, 83-101 *passim*
Bissorã, 85, 98
Boé region, 103
Boía, Moli, 95
Bolama, 83, 85, 88
Bongo (António Vicente), 115
Bongo, *soba*, 71
o *Brado Africano*, 119
Brame tribe, 89, 90
Brazil, 5, 8, 9, 10, 48-49, 51
Brazzaville, 79
Buba, 94, 95, 103
Bula, 98
Buta, Alvaro Tulante, 65, 75

Cà da Mosta, Alvise, 86
Cabinda, 61, 81
Cago Delgado, 9, 111, 122
Cabral, Amílcar, 51, 52, 90, 98, 100, 102, 103, 139
Cacanda, 94, 95
Cacheu, 83, 87, 88, 94
  river, 85, 90
Caconda, 71, 72, 74
Cadbury, William, 12
Cadornega, António de, 65
Cafuxe Cambara, 68
Caió, 96, 98
Cambambe, 67, 68
Canhabaque, 98
Cão, Diogo, 5, 62
Cape Roxo, 83, 86
Cape Verde archipelago, 1, 48, 73
  Catholic Church, 87
  discovery of, 4, 86
  economic conditions, 91-93
  nationalist movements, 99, 102
  slavery, 6, 11, 87
Caranga tribe, 109, 112
Carmona, General António, 2
Casablanca, 100
Casa dos Estudantes do Império, 29, 50, 99
Casamance, 88, 100, 102
Cassanga, Marcos, 80
Cassanga tribe, 89, 90
Cassanje kingdom, 67, 69, 70
Castro, Balthasar de, 66
Catholic action, 34, 38
Catholic Church, 21, 133-134 (*see also* Angola, Cape Verde, Moçambique, Portugal)
  missions, 30, 35, 85, 87, 108
Cavazzi, 65

Centro Associativo dos Negros de Moçambique, 50, 119
Ceuta, 3, 6, 86
Chaka, 115
Changamire, 113, 115
Chicusse, Z., 119
Childs, Gladwyn, 56
Chioko, 117
Chombe, 97, 112
Chope tribe, 109
Churó, 94, 96
Coimbra university, 2, 49
Colonial Act of 1930, 16, 18
Colonization, 7, 16, 61, 130
Comissão da Luta das Juventudes contra o Imperialismo Colonial em Angola, 78
Comité Federal Angolano do Partido Comunista Português, 78
Comité Revolucionário de Moçambique (COREMO), 121
Comité Secreto de Restauração da UDENAMO (COSERU), 121
Communist Party of Portugal, 37
Conakry, 78, 100
Conferência das Organizações Nacionalistas das Colónias Portuguesas (CONCP), 50, 100
Congo (Brazzaville), 79
Congo (Kinshasa or Léopoldville), 55, 58, 77, 80, 127
Congo kingdom, 7, 40, 53, 57, 61-65, 67, 68, 69, 70
Congo River, 5, 62, 63
Congolese kings, 61-65
Conquest, 3
  Angola, 7, 10, 53, 58
  Cape Verde, 6
  Moçambique, 8
Conselho de Líbertação de Angola, 78
Corporative Chamber, 22, 33
Correia de Sá, Salvador, 70
Corubal, 85, 97
Covilhã, Pero de, 5
Craveiro Lopes, Marshal F. H., 32
Cruz, Joaquim, 115
Cruz, Viriato da, 30, 78-79
Cuamato, 74, 75
Cuanhama, 58, 73
Cuanza river, 55, 62, 65, 66, 67, 68, 69, 71
A *Cultura*, 78
Cunene river, 55, 73
Cunha, Joaquim da Silva, 16
Cunha Leal, Francisco, 18, 19, 37
Cuór, 96, 97

Dahomey, 86
Dakar, 100
Dambarare, 113
Delagoa Bay, 105, 114, 116
Delgado, Humberto, 2, 22, 37
Dembo Ambuíla, 69
Dembos, 40, 68, 69, 70, 74, 75
Deslandes, General A. V., 32
Dias, Bartolomeu, 5, 111
Dias de Novaes, Paulo, 66-67
Diogo, 63-64
Directório Democrata Social, 36-37
Domingos, Dom, 113
Donatárias, 7, 63
Dondo, 65
De Beers Corporation, 25

Eanes, Gil, 86
Economic conditions, 24, 133 (see also Angola, Cape Verde, Guiné, Moçambique, Portugal, Príncipe, São Tomé)
Education, 29-30 (see also Angola, Moçambique, Portugal)
Edwards, Adrian, 57
Ekuikui II, King of Bailundo, 72-73
Elmina, 4, 87 (see also São Jorge da Mina)
Ennes, António, 15, 18, 116

Farim, 85, 94, 98, 101, 103
Felupe tribe, 89, 90, 94
Fernando Póo, 5
Ferreira da Costa, Eduardo, 15
First Development Plan (1955-58), 23
Frente de Acção Popular (FAP), 37
Frente de Libertação da Guiné (FLG), 101
Frente de Libertação de Moçambique (FRELIMO), 120, 121
Frente de Luta pela Independência Nacional da Guiné (FLING), 101, 102
Frente Democrática para Libertação de Angola (FDLA), 79
Frente Nacional de Libertação de Angola (FNLA), 79, 80
Frente Patriótica de Libertação Nacional (FPLN), 36, 37, 38
Frente Portuguesa de Libertação Nacional, 37
Frente Revolucionária Africana para a Independência das Colônias Portuguesas (FRAIN), 50, 100
Frente Unida Angolense (FUA), 56
Frente Unida Anti-Imperialista Popular Africana de Moçambique (FUNIPAMO), 121

Freyre, Gilberto, 47-49, 51
Front Uni de Libération de Guinée et du Cap Vert (FUL), 100
Fulacunda, 101, 103
Fula tribes, 89, 90, 94, 95, 101

Galvão, Henrique, 2, 13, 38
Gama, Vasco da, 5, 62, 111
Ganguela, 58
Gatsi Rusere, 112
Gaza, 109, 112, 115, 116, 125
Gêba, 83, 85, 90, 94, 95, 97, 103
Ghana, 13, 81
Goa, 6, 9, 22, 108, 114
Gold Coast (Ghana), 4, 87
Gomes da Costa, General Manuel, 2
Gorongosa, 117
Governo Revolucionário de Angola en Exilio (GRAE), 77, 79, 81
Grain Coast, 4
Grémio Africano, 50, 77, 119
Grumetes, 88, 97
Guarda Fiscal, 32
Guarda Nacional Republicana (GNR), 31
Guerra preta, 66, 70
Guerrilla war, 51, 127-128
    Angola, 2, 127
    Moçambique, 2, 119, 121-122, 128
    Portuguese Guiné, 2, 100-104, 128
Guidali, Bácar, 94
Guiné (see Portuguese Guiné)
Guinée, Republic of, 83, 101
Gumane, Paulo José, 121
Gungunhana, 115, 116
Gwambe, Hlomulo Chitofo, 120-121

Harris, Marvin, 13, 110
Harris, Sir John, 12
Henrique, 64
Holo kingdom, 70
Homem de Mello, Manuel José, 18-19
Huambo kingdom, 71, 72, 74
Huíla kingdom, 53, 55, 73
Humbe kingdom, 53, 71, 73, 74

Ibo, 114
Imbangala, 69
Imperialism, 124, 125
India, 5, 6, 8
Inhambane, 109, 114
Injai, Abdul, 88, 97, 98
Instituto Moçambicano, 121
Instituto Negrófilo, 119
International Labor Organization, 13

Islamic influence, 3, 35, 123 (see also Guiné, Moçambique)
Ivory Coast, 4

Jabadá, 95
Jaga tribe, 57, 63, 67, 68
João I, King of Portugal, 3
João I (Nziga a Nkuwu), 62
João II, King of Portugal, 62

Kakongo, 62
Kalundungo, José, 80
Kanina, 73
Kapango I, King of Tchiyaka, 71
Kasavubu, Joseph, 64, 81
Kassinda, Andrés, 81
Katanga, 55
Katole, 70
Kenya African National Union (KANU), 120
Kibiriti Diwami, 119
Kilwa, 6, 111, 113
Kinara, 102
Kinkouzou, 80
Kissama kingdom, 66, 67, 68, 69
Kounzika, Emmanuel, 79

Labery, Henri, 99
Labor, 15, 39-40, 130-131
    code, 12
    conditions, 13, 15, 25, 131
    contract labor, 40
    emigration to South Africa, 110
    English condemnation of, 12, 13
    liberto, 12
    report by Galvão, 2, 13, 38
Lake Niassa, 105, 110, 115, 121
Lançados, 87
Law of Economic Reconstruction (1935-50), 23
Legião Portuguesa, 31
Leópoldville (Kinshasa), 76, 78, 79, 80, 81
Liahuca, José, 81
Libertos, 12
Liga Africana, 49
Liga Nacional Africana, 50, 77
Lisbon, 2, 49, 50
Loango, 62
Lobito, 55
Lobo clan, 117
Lourenço Marques, 105-119
Lumumba, Patrice, 81
Lunda kingdom, 70, 72, 74
Lusotropicology, 47-49, 51, 85, 110, 126, 135-136, 139

Maconde tribe, 119
Maconga tribe, 110
Macua tribe, 108, 110, 117, 118
Madagascar, 111
Madeira islands, 4, 21
Maguiguana, 116
Makunde, 66
Malacca, 10
Malange, 40, 55, 57, 75, 76, 78
Malawi, 105, 109, 120
Malindi, 5
Mandinga tribe, 89, 90, 94, 95, 96, 101
Manica district, 109, 112, 113, 117
Manjaco tribe 89, 90, 96, 97, 101, 103
Manjacaze, 116
Manso Paiva, 62
Manuel, King of Portugal, 5, 63, 113
Massangano, 67, 115
Matamba kingdom, 67, 68, 69, 70
Matuzianhe, 112
Mavura, 113
Mavura Mhande, 114
Mbandi Ngola Kiluanje, King of Angola, 66
Mbanza Kongo (São Salvador), 62, 64
Mbemba a Nzinga (Affonso I), 62
Mbula Matadi, 64
Mbundu kingdom, 65, 69
Mbunda, David J. M., 121
Mbwila, 65, 70
Memba, 118
Mendes das Neves Monsignor, 35
A Mensagem, 30, 78
Mmole, Mathew, 121
Moçambique, 1, 6, 105-122 passim, 139-141
    African refugees, 121
    British claims, 116
    Catholic Church, 108, 110
    conquest of, 8
    economic conditions, 24, 40, 105, 107-108
    education, 30
    ethnic groups, 108-110
    geography, 105
    Islamic influence, 108, 111, 114, 117
    labor, 13, 110
    nationalist movements, 2, 21, 40, 50, 52, 105, 119-122
    pacification, 14, 115-118
    Portuguese emigration, 9
    Protestant church, 108
Moçambique African National Congress (MANCO), 121
Moçambique African National Union (MANU), 119, 121

Moçambique Channel, 105
Moçambique Company, 9
Moçambique district, 117
Moçambique island, 111, 113
Moçambique Maconde Union, 120
Moçambique Revolutionary Council
    (MORECO), 121
Moló Mussá, 95
Mombasa, 5, 6, 111, 113, 120
Mompataz, Régulo of, 93
Mondlane, Eduardo, 52, 119, 120, 121
Mondlane, Janet, 121
Monhes, 108
Monomotapa, 8, 109, 112, 113, 114
Monteiro, Armindo, 16
Moreira, Adriano, 17
Morocco, 86, 113
Mouvement de Libération des Iles du Cap
    Vert (MLICV), 101
Movimento Anti-Colonista (MAC), 50
Movimento de Acção Revolucionário, 37
Movimento de Libertação da Guiné (MLG),
    100
Movimento de Libertação da Guiné e Cabo
    Verde (MLGCV), 100
Movimento de Resistência Republicana, 37
Movimento de Unidade Democrático, 38
Movimento para a Independência Nacional
    da Guiné Portuguesa, 99
Movimento Popular de Libertação de An-
    gola (MPLA), 75, 77, 78, 79, 81
Mpanzu a Nzinga, 62, 64
Mussolini, Benito, 1, 31
Mutu-ya-Kevela, Bailundo king, 73
Muxuebata, Jorge, 64

Nalú tribe, 88, 89, 90
Nano wars, 74
National Assembly, Portuguese, 13, 22, 33,
    116
Nationalism, 43-52, 134-136
    African nationalism, 2, 49-52, 84, 125,
        127, 134-136
    Angolan rebellion, 2, 3, 7, 17, 21, 22, 38,
        53, 74-77
    Portuguese nationalism, 43-49, 126, 134-
        136
Nationalist movements (see Angola, Cape
    Verde, Guiné, Moçambique)
Native Assistance Code, 15, 132
Ndongo kingdom, 56, 57, 58, 67, 68-69, 70
Ndulu kingdom, 56, 72
Ndunduma I, 73
Négritude, 50, 126
Nekaka, Manuel Barros, 80

Netherlands, 6, 10, 65, 69, 70, 87
Neto, Agostinho, 30, 52, 75, 78-79
Nevinson, Henry W., 12
New State, 2, 15-16, 18, 21, 23, 31, 33-34,
    36 38, 41, 47, 49, 89, 127, 131, 134
Ngola, King, 65, 67, 70
Ngola Ari, 70
Ngola Kanini, 70
Ngola a Nzinga, 65
Ngola Nzinga Mbandi, 68
Ngoni, 109, 112, 115
Ngwizako-Ngwizani a Kongo, 80
Nhacra, 96, 98
Niassa, 110, 117, 122
Niassa Company, 9, 118
Nkoje, 65
Nkuwu a Nitinu, 62
North Atlantic Treaty Organization
    (NATO), 3, 32-33, 41, 128
Norton de Matos, José, 15
Nova Lisboa, 8, 61, 73, 76
Novo Lamego (Gabu), 85, 103
Ntinu Mini a Lukeni, 62
Ntolela or Manicongo, 62
Numa II, King of Bailundo, 73
Nuno, Dom Duarte, 36
Nzinga a Nkuwu (João I), 62, 64
Nzinga Mbandi (Anna de Souza Nzinga),
    68, 69, 70

Oio, 89, 96, 97
Ormuz, 6
Organic Charter, 16
Ornellas, Ayres d', 15
Overseas Reform Act, 16
Ovimbundu, 53, 56-58, 71-74
Owen, W. F., 116

Pacification, 6, 53, 59-60, 71, 88, 93-103,
    115-118
Pais, Sidónio, 1
Paiva Couceiro, Henrique de, 15
Palanca, 94
Papel tribe, 89-91, 93-98, 101
Partido Africano da Independência da
    Guiné e Cabo Verde (PAIGC), 99,
    100, 102, 103, 139
Partido Communista Angolano (PCA), 78
Partido de Luta Unida dos Africanos de
    Angola (PLUA), 78
Partido Democrático de Angola (PDA), 79
Partido Pro-Angola, 77
Paté Mamadú, 94-96
Pedro, son of Affonso I, 63
Pedro VIII, king of Angola, 80

Pelundo, 98
Pia de Saxe-Cobourg, Princess Maria, 36
Pinto Bull, Benjamin and Jaime, 101
Pereira clan, 117
Pijiguiti, 100
Pinto de Andrade, Joaquim, 75
Polícia Internacional e Defesa do Estado
    (PIDE), 31
Polícia de Segurança Pública (PSP), 31
Polícia Judiciária, 32
Portugal:
    administration overseas, 3, 10, 15-18, 22,
        27-28, 33, 132
    army of, 1, 31, 32, 36, 41, 92, 94, 117
    banks in, 24, 26, 92
    Catholic Church, 21, 31, 33-35, 36, 41,
        127
    censorship in, 28
    colonial bureaucracy, 10, 27, 33, 131
    colonial policy, 14-17, 25, 27, 31, 48, 51,
        123, 130-132
    "corporative state," 23, 132
    economic conditions, 2, 23-27, 39, 127,
        132
    education, 29
    geography, 45
    imperial mystique, 2, 46-47, 123, 128,
        134-136
    industrialist families, 25, 35-36
    labor, 27, 31, 38-39
    landowners in, 25, 26
    monarchism, 36
    nationalism, 43-49, 126, 134-136
    opposition in, 21, 22, 28-29, 31-32, 34-
        35, 36-38
    reform measures, 3, 13, 14, 16, 17, 60
    Revolution of 1910, 14
    social stratification, 27
    students, 22, 31, 38
Portuguese companies, 9
Portuguese emigration, 39
Portuguese expansion, 3-6
Portuguese Guiné, 1, 4, 83-104 passim, 138-
    139
    African refugees, 102
    conquest of, 86-89
    economic conditions, 91-93
    ethnic groups, 85, 89-90
    geography, 83, 85
    gold trade, 6
    Islamic influence, 89
    labor, 99, 100
    nationalist movements, 40, 50, 99-103
    pacification, 88, 93-103
    slavery, 11

Portuguese Society of Writers, 28-29
Portuguese State of India, 113
Praia, 91, 102
Prazos, 8-9, 114-117
Prester John, 4, 5, 62
Primavera, 76
Primo de Rivera, Miguel, 2
Prince Henry, 3, 4, 46, 86, 123
Príncipe, 1, 5, 138-139
    economic conditions, 92-93
Protestant church, 35 (see also Angola,
    Moçambique)

Querimba, 114
Quibaxe, 76

Racial harmony, 11
Rassemblement Démocratique Africain de
    la Guinée Portugaise (RDAG), 101
Ravenstein, Ernst Georg, 62
Refugees, 59-60, 80, 100, 102, 127
Regimento, 63
Resistance to Portuguese, 2, 49, 63-74, 84,
    93-103, 127
Rhodes, Cecil, 14, 116
Rio Grande (river), 83, 86
Roberto, Holden, 52, 79-80
Rodrigues, José Honório, 48-49
Rodrigues, Admiral Sarmento, 32
Ross, Edward Alsworth, 12

Sá de Bandeira, 12, 55, 61
Salazar, António de Oliveira, 2, 15-19, 21-
    23, 28, 29, 32-34, 36, 41, 47, 79,
    126-128, 131
Salvaterra de Magos, 73-74
Sambel Nhantá, 97
"Santa Maria," 2, 38, 79
Santos, Marcelino dos, 50
São Domingos, 101, 103
São João Baptista d'Ajudá, 86
São Jorge da Mina, 4, 10, 87 (see also El-
    mina)
São Salvador, 7, 58, 62, 76
São Tiago, 87, 91
São Tomé, 1, 5, 62, 63, 65, 83-104, 138-
    139
    economic conditions, 92-93
    slavery, 11, 12
Save river, 105, 109, 110
Savimbi, Jonas, 81
Sebastião, King of Portugal, 9, 63, 113, 123
Second Development Plan (1959–64), 23
Sena, 112, 114, 115, 117
Senegal, 84, 91, 98, 100, 101, 103

Senegal river, 4, 86
Shama, 4, 87
Shanganas, 115
shibalos, 13
Sierra Leone, 4
Sindicato Nacional dos Empregados do Comércio e da Indústria, 99
Slave Coast, 4
Slavery, 4, 6, 11-12, 48, 55-56, 130-131
Soares de Resende, Bishop, 35
Sofala, 8, 111, 113, 115
Soshangane, 109, 115
South Africa, 2, 13, 41, 60, 105, 107, 109, 128
South-west Africa, 55, 58, 74
Southern Rhodesia, 2, 41, 105, 107, 119, 128
Soyo kingdom, 68
Spain, 2, 8, 10, 31
Sports and Recreation Association, 99
Suzana, 100

Tanganyïka, 112, 118, 121, 122
Tanganyika African National Union (TANU), 120
Taty, Alexandre, 81
Tchiyaka, 71, 72
Tchyoka, 73
Teixeira Pinto, João, 88, 97, 98
Teixeira Pinto, Luís, 27
Tete, 113-115
Tomás, Ádmiral Américo, 33
Tongas tribe, 108-109, 112, 115
Trade, 87, 113, 123-124
  gold trade, 3, 4, 5, 8, 11, 111, 123-124
  Muslim merchants, 5, 7, 10
  slave, 5, 7, 11, 55-57, 62, 65-71, 77, 87, 94, 123
  spice, 4-6, 10, 123-124
Transvaal, 109
Tribes:
  Angola, 56-58
  Guiné, 89-90
  Moçambique, 108-110
Tristão, Nuno, 86
Tunis, 50, 78, 100

Umzila, 115
União Africana de Moçambique Independente (UNAMI), 120, 121
União das Populações de Angola (UPA), 76, 77
União das Populações da Guiné (UPG), 101
União das Populações do Norte de Angola (UPNA), 80
União Democrática Nacional de Moçambique (UDENAMO), 119, 121
União Democrática Nacional de Monomotapa (UDENAMO-Monomotapa), 121
União Nacional, 22, 33
União Nacional dos Trabalhadores da Guiné (UNTG), 100
Union des Resortissants de la Guinée Portugaise (URGP), 101
United Arab Republic, 121
United Nations, 17, 25, 41, 59, 60, 75, 77, 81, 107, 128, 133
  General Assembly, 3, 128
  Security Council, 3, 101, 128
  Trusteeship Committee, 2, 3
United States (of America), 3, 41
  in Africa, 41
  economic interests, 60
  U.S.-owned Cabinda Gulf Company, 24

Valente, M. G., 119
Varela, 96, 101
Vicente, António (Bongo), 115
Vieira, Luandino, 29

Waq-Wags, 112

Zambeze river, 9, 55, 105, 110, 113-115, 117
Zambézia Company, 9, 117
Zambézia district, 117, 122
Zambia, 55, 58, 105, 109
Zanj, 112
Zanzibar, 111
Ziguinchor, 88, 95
Zumbo, 117